WALK
AMONG THE
DRAGONFLIES

WALK AMONG THE DRAGONFLIES

How Leaders Streamline Efficiencies Through Process Improvement

DR. JORDAN THURSTON

EVOLVELIKEADRAGONFLY.COM

Published by Evolve Like a Dragonfly LLC
For more resources, slides, and educational materials, go to:
evolvelikeadragonfly.com

First paperback edition published 2024

ISBN 979-8-218-22329-8 (paperback)
ISBN 979-8-218-28296-7 (ebook)

Library of Congress Control Number: 2023917700

Cover design: Steve Thurston
Cover illustration: Shutterstock®
Interior illustrations: Joshua Thurston
Back cover photo: John Emerson

Printed in the United States of America

10 9 8 7 6 5 4 3 2 1

To those who have held onto great ideas for far too long and never brought them to fruition and those who want to make a difference in the world around them.

CONTENTS

Foreword

The Dragonfly Construct is the product of an enquiring mind. A mind that relishes and thrives on the challenges of change in life and the corporate world. Change is the only constant. If there's one thing that history teaches us, it is that unless both people and the organizations they serve are constantly adapting and innovating, they quickly become obsolete. Jordan uses the Dragonfly Construct to challenge both the old-timer and the apprentice alike to get out of their comfort zones and be ready to explore, innovate, and adapt to stay well ahead of the curve. *Walk Among the Dragonflies* is a highly readable common sense book born out of personal experience, observation, and success. It will quickly resonate with those who are eager to succeed in a career in business or to thrive in the corporate world. It will encourage, motivate, and inspire them to see their role in a new way and to consider the challenges they face in any organization as opportunities to be seized and enjoyed, not chores to be avoided.

Ambassador Dennis Ignatius
April 10, 2024

Preface

Process improvement has always been part of my life. I look at processes as puzzles and the individual steps within them as the pieces. When I was younger, I would write areas of opportunity and solutions on napkins wherever I went and give them to the manager... who most likely lobbed them in the trash after I left. However, the ability to pick up on things that most people glance over has become a power tool in my belt and has served me well in my career.

My journey into the business world started on a hot summer day when I visited my family in Kuala Lumpur, Malaysia, when I was 16. I remember stopping for coffee at Starbucks with my grandpa and navigating the crowds to find a table. The one we found had a newspaper left behind and opened to an article, 'Ten Reasons to Get into Business.' I recall reading it and immediately falling in love with the topics covered and wanting to explore further the thought of pursuing a career in business. Fast forward, we were on a flight to Singapore to visit family, and in my seat-back pocket was Kiplinger's Finance magazine with an article on reasons to get into finance and the general industry. Call it luck, an intervention from

God, or just some lazy person who left their magazine on the plane, but it was the ultimate impetus that pushed me to dive into business.

Process improvement, or re-engineering, is vital for your future success and that of your company. As technology and regulatory landscapes adapt, so should our processes and the way we look at the activities we perform day-to-day. Like a dragonfly, we must be able to move in multiple directions and continuously improve to meet the demands of management, stakeholders, auditors, and government agencies. It's imperative to constantly look for ways to streamline processes from a Lean perspective. I challenge everyone reading this book to act and look around your current workplace and teams and propose one solution to better an existing process. Process improvement has become a common theme in my day-to-day operations, work, and community. Like our careers, processes undergo a metamorphosis as perspectives and mindsets change. Like a dragonfly, we must continue to learn, adapt, and grow the world around us.

This book was written to serve as a tool for managers and employees to challenge the status quo of how strategy is created and implemented within a corporation and streamline efficiencies to derive a new format for strategic management and process improvement. Just as I have transformed my life and career like a dragonfly, I hope this book has the same impact on you.

CHAPTER 1

Transform and Evolve
Like a Dragonfly

Ideas are powerful. Sometimes mind-blowing. Little neurons in your brain bounce against each other, building momentum as they construct concepts, thoughts, notions, and impressions. This roadmap of spontaneous, reflexive ideas or suggestions has the power to trigger creativity, spark innovation, and create those "Aha!" moments.

You can't anticipate ideas; they surround you as they thirst for an outlet. Problems, ingenious or injurious, will arise in many ways and burn through well-planned situations that have been laid out in a logistical and strategic arrangement that we call axioms. But what happens when opportunistic and transformational ideas cease, interrupted by obstructive circumstances? What happens when an issue that inhibits our ability to implement a sound solution arises? What happens when we are left feeling stranded in a magnitude of vines that are choking our ideas and solutions for a better process? What happens when we encounter a process or procedure, strategic vision, or a forward-moving thoroughfare of plans and sentiments towards a complex position and are left stranded with a field guide missing the most crucial blueprint: good judgment and wisdom?

This perilous moment, where an idea breaks and falls apart from internal or external factors and then rises out of the ashes towards process improvement and transformational lifecycle, is what I call "The Dragonfly Construct," a process that breathes life into our critical and strategic thinking process.

As I walked in my backyard on a warm summer day with my Australian Shepherd, Mochi, I was taking in the sunshine when I realized I was surrounded by dragonflies. I was enamored by the feeling of walking among the dragonflies as they soared around me carefree amongst a potential threat. I immediately began to think about the journey of a dragonfly and linked it to personal transformation. Like humans, dragonflies undergo difficult stages of their lives that, while different, can mimic comparable situations. The ability to overcome these stages, challenges, and threats in an ever-changing ecosystem is not easy, and many factors can limit growth; however, they develop a level of expertise to thrive. There are three stages in the lifecycle of a dragonfly: egg, larva, and adult. At each stage, developments are made to better position the dragonfly to continue growing. Overlaying the lifecycle of one's career helps paint a more profound link between the two.

Years ago, and long before giving it a fancy name, I developed the concept of the "Dragonfly Construct" while working in retail management. I'll share a little more about that later in the book. At one point, I took it with me into the financial industry. I can confidently bear witness to the success stories of applying this construct to career advancement, not solely for myself but for many others. Guaranteed career growth may not always follow a one-size-fits-all model, but following the concepts and ideas outlined in this book can help you understand your role and the processes that impact your team or company. Sure, anyone can change a process, but how we do it affects not only the process but often those connected to it and the potential to add further value to our team and company.

I created this construct to challenge the status quo of how strategy is developed and implemented within a corporation and to streamline efficiencies to derive a new format for strategic management and process improvement.

The Dragonfly Construct

Dragonflies are often seen as a symbol of transformation, and a lot can be learned from their lifecycle and push to grow and adapt to their surroundings. When we start a new job, we are new to the company, its environment, culture, and our role's inner workings. We are often seen as being "underwater" or treading water to learn a new skill set, understand company-based processes, find where we fit, etc. At this stage, it's important to absorb as much as possible regarding the environment, behaviors, management, and other vital areas that will lay the groundwork for our success. The Dragonfly Construct focuses on the first six months at a new job and helps add immediate value to engaging and further transforming a company's processes.

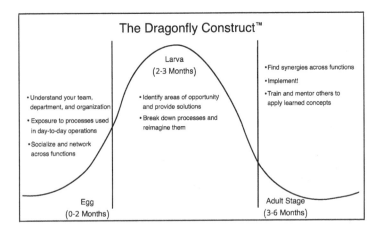

The Egg Stage

Starting off in the egg stage is akin to starting at a new job; we learn the environment and understand how to perform the roles and responsibilities. This stage typically lasts anywhere from 0-2 months and is the most suitable time to self-integrate into the company's culture and where we fit in the mix. This is the perfect time to network with those in varying and more senior positions. Don't be afraid to pull the "new joiner" card to facilitate conversations. What worked well for me was setting meetings with managing directors, or people responsible for entire organizations, and learning about their roles, pain points, and tips that helped them get to where they are. I also asked for personal recommendations on team members they felt would be ideal to speak with regarding the pain points and continued to set up meetings. I was able to collate many of these points and integrate solutions via sub-functions on my team to help address them. While everyone's role differs, you can drive your career and adapt your function to take on additional responsibilities, which will aid your growth as a leader. When companies promote, they typically look for employees who are able to not only lead well but also think outside the box to address current issues and pain points.

As you network around your company, specifically with your department and team, look out for any areas of opportunity that pique your interest, jot them down, and save them for later. By identifying areas of improvement or gaps early on, we place ourselves in a better position to build a strategic roadmap and develop a function that better considers the existing landscape and the proposed end state. The best starting point is talking to stakeholders and prior team members to understand key pain points. This is something that should be done shortly after taking the position. Like the dragonfly, during a specific timeframe in the role, we undergo an iteration of metamorphosis. As we understand the role and organization and continue to grow, we can network outside of our core group of stakeholders and identify synergies across departments, organizations, divisions, etc.

The Larva Stage

Post-metamorphosis, the next stage is the larva stage, in which the dragonfly seeks higher ground to avoid predators and thoroughly understands the environment, deriving a survival strategy. In this stage, we are constantly growing in our roles and learning from mentors either sought out personally or assigned by the firm. This is the time, roughly between months 2 and 3, that we want to refer to the process improvement notes jotted down earlier in the egg stage and put them into effect. This is a crucial part of the construct as it drives the value we're adding through the addition, removal, or modification of steps in a process.

As we begin to piece together and examine workflows, take a step back and try to understand the process's current objective. It is vital to fully know the purpose to be able to modify or remove steps and ensure that the message isn't lost or compound confusion for those following it. Most companies have change management guidelines or how processes can be changed, their frequency, and how they are communicated. Be aware that other teams or organizations within the company may leverage the same process, so making changes without first knowing the scale can cause issues and have the opposite effect that we are trying to have. Once we've been made aware of the end-to-end scope of a process, it's time to act.

From my conversations with others on this, the line I hear most often is that an idea is "too simple" and that "someone must have already thought of it, so that's why it's not implemented." While this may be true, a fresh perspective often does wonders and may not have been considered.

While working for a large video game retailer, I took regular trips to various stores in my district and observed many different methods being utilized in employee training. As a result of my observations, I drafted a small talent development plan to implement across the stores and emailed it to the CEO. I shared this insight with a few people within my district, including my manager, who told me it was a waste and too simple of an idea to get a response because it had likely already been considered. As I hit send, I sat back and thought I had done one of two things... either something incredible... or I was about to get fired for significantly jumping the chain of command to voice an area of opportunity and a solution. After 40 excruciatingly long minutes, I got a reply saying, "Thank you Jordan, I appreciate your input! I will discuss your input with [names of his leadership team], who manage our US leadership development." Over several weeks, I worked with their leadership team to implement some aspects of my proposal. When this happened, I was in awe. How could something so simple not have been brought up? Was the way I analyzed situations different? This train of thought has stuck with me as I continue implementing process changes where I'm constantly met with "no one has ever done it this way" or "if it's not broken, there is no need to fix it."

Often, leadership can underestimate that their work could be done better or more efficiently. Sometimes, all it takes is to challenge the status quo, highlight areas of opportunity, and provide solutions. It's as simple as that. It's always essential to propose your ideas because the worst thing that can happen is your management telling you no. However, if it's something that hasn't been done before, congratulations! You have successfully identified an area of opportunity and can now take the call to action to implement it. There are many times that individuals know what's wrong, but they choose to do nothing due to the following:

1. They don't have a voice within their department or at the organizational level
2. They are complacent in their role and don't care
3. Are stuck in the mindset of "it's always been done this way"
4. They have a negative perception about the change
5. They don't have enough experience to notice or understand that a process or procedure is faulty

I was talking to John, a friend from high school, and he shared a story about when he was hired to come in and make internal changes—changes that were supposed to be improvements to processes and procedures that the CEO felt were faulty within his organization. The CEO had a laundry list of items that he had written down on a piece of paper that was folded multiple times into a small square. The CEO said, "Get this fixed as soon as possible," handing John the folded paper. As the CEO walked away, he looked back at John and yelled, "You have a month to get these issues fixed, and I want to start seeing results ASAP." Not sure what "I want to start seeing results" truly implied, John envisioned the worst nightmare of his career, fixing a list of areas and issues he had no input or knowledge of. John worked directly with the CEO for a couple of days, sitting in meetings and reviewing how the CEO wanted things to run, as he pointed to specific people as the culprits for each item on the list.

Four weeks into John's job, he just happened to be walking the building hallways and bumped into a gentleman who clearly knew John's name. As the gentleman approached John, he introduced himself as a board director and shared how they had talked about John at their meeting just a few minutes ago. In fact, they were having a board meeting in the other room, and they were all taking a break. This board director told John how excited he was that things would finally change and improve. He said to John, "At our last board meeting, we told him [the CEO] that he needed to hire someone that had the right leadership, skillset, and talent to come in and research why there is a lack of communication, motivation, trust, and why there are so many issues that are affecting the organization and the employees." The director joked by saying to go ahead and ruffle as many feathers as you need to figure this out. This particular director might have spoken a little too much, maybe because he did not trust the CEO, or maybe there was something deeper he could not share. Still, he did mention that the CEO had a lot of weaknesses and that John was the key person to come in and provide a professional point of view of strength to help the CEO identify issues and help lead in the areas where the CEO was underperforming.

This conversation was an eye-opener for John. The board director was painting a picture in a particular light, a somewhat negative portrayal of the CEO with a positive outlook of potential change. Yet John's interactions and requests from the CEO were much different in perspective. As weeks passed, all meetings between John and the CEO stopped. There were no phone calls or emails to John about anything. It was as if the CEO was ghosting John. Every time John tried to set up a meeting with the CEO, it was denied, or John was informed that the CEO was too busy and told to continue researching and working on fixing the issues. It became apparent very quickly that John would end up sitting in his office week after week, fulfilling a position that at first looked like a dire need directly for change and improvement requests from the CEO, but now it was a dead-end position. It was as if the CEO hired John to fulfill the demands of the board of directors, but now that the board meeting was over, there was no need for John or his input.

John finally sat down with the CEO to share his findings almost three months later. John's research surfaced many detailed problems, the vast majority pointing at the CEO being at fault. It was hard for John to share this; he was putting his new job and career on the line by telling the person who hired him to fix things that the problem all along was the leadership at the top—the CEO. The CEO got very defensive with John's results from his research, dismissing every single one of John's findings. John gave him a 48-page document that provided all the evidence, solutions, and recommendations for mitigating them. Many included easy ways to make

WALK AMONG THE DRAGONFLIES – 15

improvements or changes that John felt would turn the organization around in six months. As John left that meeting, he left a copy of the document with the CEO, hoping these areas would be addressed.

After two years in that position, John decided to leave. The CEO had yet to address or consider all of the items on his document. The issues were never discussed again after John presented them to the CEO. Sadly, over time, John could clearly see that the CEO needed more experience to be the leader this organization deserved and that the CEO could not handle the execution of John's input.

As John finished sharing this story with me, he mentioned that the organizational culture had become very toxic, and the CEO always had this "my way or the highway" condescending attitude towards employees, their ideas, and their work. John looked me straight in the eye and, unfortunately, said that what he believed to have been his dream job at this organization quickly turned into a bizarre, micromanaged, and manipulative opportunity from a leader who was often pretentious and arrogant, lacking in empathy, and intolerant to accept people with differing opinions. This led to poor performance as a CEO and poor performance from employees.

All it takes is to raise your hand and share your ideas. This will immediately put you on management's radar as someone who can think outside the box and has critical and strategic thinking skills. If you see an area of opportunity, say something. Chances are, no one has said anything before.

The Adult Stage

The final stage is the adult stage, where dragonflies learn to be adaptive. They can fly in six directions at a moment's notice to avoid danger, seek shelter, and even catch smaller insects for food—all while learning how to live post-metamorphic transformation. In corporate, it often feels like we are pulled in six different directions between business-as-usual and additional tasks through stretch goals or wearing multiple hats.

After hitting a certain point in a role, your management or other teams will see your performance and come to you with new opportunities to take on additional work on top of your primary job. This is done to drive collaboration and growth across the firm further, also known as stretch assignments. These stretch assignments are essential as they introduce us to new technologies, teams, and processes that can be further integrated into current responsibilities. After 3-6 months in the role, our grasp on day-to-day operations and our role in the team should be well understood. After combining knowledge and experience from the previous stages, your ability to look beyond our scope of responsibilities also allows you to find synergies across different teams and functions. At this point, we can see what is being done well or where areas for opportunity are present and seek to integrate them into our processes or provide solutions for other teams' processes that we may have influence over.

After six months, the dragonfly dies off, but that doesn't mean your career or processes will follow suit. It has experienced a lot through its journey and contributed to creating the next generation of dragonflies to walk the earth. This is the time to take the knowledge you have learned and apply it through the Dragonfly Construct and begin to mentor those around you, both internal and external to your company. Understanding process management or re-engineering in today's environment is a significant skill set to obtain and can be applied to any existing role. As your company's economic and social landscapes adapt and shift, so should your processes – and all it takes is someone willing to step up and do the work. Throughout my career, professionally and academically, I have mentored and continue to mentor students and professionals to build their brand and become experts in the process improvement or continuous improvement space.

Putting It All Together

Driving process improvements in a global company can be terrifying and daunting; however, there is a bigger reward when it impacts not only yourself and the company but also the local community. When I think of an end-to-end process of the Dragonfly Construct that yielded great results, it was when I was asked to run the Jr. Business Analyst program at one of the largest financial institutions in the world. At that time, it was a program that had been established for roughly three years that partnered with local school districts to bring high school seniors into the office to give them real-world experience and bridge the gap between the theory learned in the classroom and the practical side of the workforce. It had great success in finding top talent and giving the students the necessary exposure to what it's like to work for a global bank, which resulted in many of them being hired after graduation. When I took the reins, I saw an opportunity to expand this further... but how could I, an Assistant Vice President, remotely have an impact? It was already a robust process within a single organization of the bank but with little to no marketing or awareness.

As I entered the egg stage, I began to socialize the program and met with others who ran similar programs for college analysts or coding boot camps to get an idea of how they were able to expand and grow. In this case, I leveraged the "new" card to ensure I covered all my bases before putting together a proposal. At this stage, I began to gain exposure to the different processes and subprocesses involved in this large-scale, enterprise-wide program and saw where I could improve them within my own space. In the larva stage, I began to draft up these areas of opportunities and the solutions to address gaps and have a sustainable process and program. I even drafted the processes on a whiteboard and ran through each phase to see where they could be consolidated or removed to drive efficiency. Some of these included how to quickly vet and onboard school districts, attract other managers and senior leaders to get on board and participate in the program, and ensure students had actual, impactful projects to last them the entire school year. Finally, I entered the adult stage. I compiled my notes and proposal, citing quantitative and qualitative data of the recent cohorts who participated in the program, and identified who I needed to speak with to implement it. There was a town hall with the head of operations & technology, and at the end of it, he asked everyone to reach out if they had ideas, concerns, or general feedback. I took advantage of it. I immediately met with his administrative assistant and secured a 30-minute slot on his calendar. When the day came, I was nervous but excited and motivated. I joined our internal meeting application and waited. He joined! He informed me that I was the only one who reached out to him, and we proceeded with introductions and learning more about his role. Toward the end of our conversation, I made the pitch. I wanted to expand the program globally. I shared my insights and their impact on the company and the development of the next-generation workforce. I stated that high school graduates were an untapped market that few companies were exploiting. From there, the rest is history. The program, which has been in place for over eight years now, has expanded outside of the small organization in Texas to New York and London, with more sites to be added this year.

When I embarked on my journey, I didn't know how to go about it. Through the concepts in the Dragonfly Construct, I could plan, prepare, and learn about how others were implementing similar programs and adapted these processes accordingly to meet the needs of my program systemically and methodically. Never in a million years would I have thought that I'd have an impact at my company and in the community, providing high school students in Title 1 or low-income school districts a platform for learning, growth, and development. It goes to show you that no matter where you sit in a company, YOU can drive your career and be impactful. While you may not start a high school internship program (which you most definitely should), even the smallest of processes can significantly impact the world around you.

The Dragonfly Construct creates immediate value for your team, department, and organization by having a fresh pair of eyes to identify areas of opportunity and re-engineer existing processes. By identifying areas of improvement or gaps early on, we place ourselves in a better position to build strategic roadmaps and develop a function that better considers the existing landscape and the proposed end state. No matter where you work or what you do, whether retail or corporate, you can make a difference, implement new processes, and identify new areas for improvement. And it's not only at work. The Dragonfly Construct can be used to improve processes at home too. You can take this to teach your family members and friends to improve the processes in their everyday lives.

Case Study 1 – The Dragonfly Construct

Audience: Organizations (offsite activity or general team building exercise) and Individuals (personal, high school, or college class activity).

Purpose: Using Chapter 1: Transform and Evolve like a Dragonfly, select one area of opportunity (personal or work-related) and run it through the Dragonfly Construct. This exercise will get you in the process improvement mindset and help find unique ways to challenge the status quo.

Structure: 500-1,500-word analysis

Process:
Step 1. The Egg Stage

1. Based on your understanding of your team, department, or organization, identify one area of opportunity within a process
   a. What is the purpose of the process?
   b. Is it a national, regional, or global process?

Step 2. The Larva Stage

1. Provide a minimum of one solution
   a. How would you solve the problem identified?
2. Reimagine
   a. Reimagine the process end-to-end; what would

you change to improve the process flow? And why?

Step 3. The Adult Stage

1. Understand the interdependencies within the process
   a. Are other teams using it?
   b. If you change something, will it impact anyone?
2. Will this change require approval from anyone? (manager, spouse, significant other, friend, family)
3. What is the timeframe to implement the change to the process?

Step 4. Detailed Analysis

Provide a detailed write-up with the area of opportunity, potential solution, analysis of the Dragonfly Construct, and proposed execution time.

Be sure to include the following:

1. The process you are improving
2. What is the issue, and what is your solution to resolve it?
3. Are there other teams dependent on this process?
4. How long it will take to implement the change to the process?

Step 5. Check Your Understanding

Based on your analysis, include responses to the below questions:

1. Is this the first time you improved a process? If not, what are some of the experiences you've had?
2. What made you decide to select the area of opportunity?
3. What was the reason for choosing the proposed solution(s)?
4. What happens if you encounter an issue after you roll out the process?
5. How do you think you can apply the Dragonfly Construct to other areas?

CHAPTER 2

The Importance of a Good Mindset

A good mindset is critical to developing one's personal life and career. Many different mindsets exist today – growth, creativity, and confidence, to name a few. Some people choose to pair them together or use them individually, as there is no wrong way to utilize them. A good mindset can be the catalyst for existing processes, creating contagious opportunities and inspiring and motivating others to take action. In contrast, a bad mindset can impede any growth. Mindsets are developed, learned, and absorbed through daily interactions, reading books, watching motivational speakers, or observing how one conducts business in various situations. No matter your upbringing or outlook on life, just like one innovates a process, you can innovate how you handle challenging situations, work conflicts, or even receive additional workloads. Someone can look up at the sky and see its bleak, dreary nature and another person beside them can see it as a beautiful day full of opportunity. A good mindset unlocks opportunities and opens doors. If someone approached you and told you to do better, would you think they had a positive or negative mindset?

The Pre-Flight Mindset

Before dragonflies take their first flight, they must first learn to survive the new world surrounding them. Dragonflies embark on a journey of life and death as they make their way through the lifecycle. While it's not a battle between life and death at work, starting a new position may feel like fighting for your life to fit in, learn the culture, and ultimately understand the role. This can be overwhelming for many, but laying out your game plan can initially set you up for success. This is where the Pre-Flight Mindset comes in. It allows you to focus on what matters when starting a new job, which gives a good impression that demonstrates your personality and ability to perform what's needed.

1. To implement this, you need to first explore your environment. This entails meeting your team and other colleagues to learn about the work you'll be doing and how it impacts other teams.

2. As you continue to explore, it's essential to over-communicate by asking questions and clarifying what is assigned to you. Understanding the background of your work will allow you to identify areas of

opportunity later and provide potential solutions.

3. Finally, it's time to deliver results. When you are assigned work and given a deadline, it's imperative that you do everything you can to deliver either ahead of schedule or on time. This will ultimately pave the way for you to build your brand, which I'll share more about at the end of this chapter.

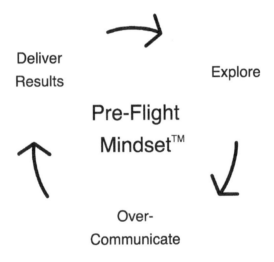

The Pre-Flight Mindset can be applied directly to the Egg Stage of the Dragonfly Construct. As you find your footing and venture into your new role and company, you begin your pre-flight journey. Soon, you'll be soaring like a dragonfly in no time.

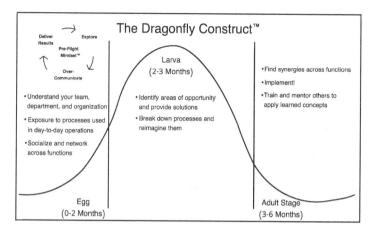

When I started as an Assistant Vice President, I was in charge of the vendor transformation function. This included managing two vendors, ensuring they met their contractual obligations or service level agreements, and hosting weekly and monthly operational reviews. At first, I didn't know much about vendor management —I always tell people you never wake up one day as a child and want to become a vendor manager; you fall into it. To learn more about the role, I explored my surroundings, found other teams that were running similar functions, and performed market research. And believe me, I over-communicated, sometimes too much. It allowed me to find a balance between asking clarifying questions and believing in myself to do what needed to be done. After building up self-confidence and an understanding of the role, I began to deliver results. Whether I raised my hand to take on more work or was assigned projects, I always delivered them on time, contributing to my brand. This allowed me to get promoted to Vice President two years later.

The User Metamorphosis Mindset

This is a new spin on driving user engagement, product adoption, and user experience. Often, we want to drive change and process improvement immediately, but for others, it may take time. To implement this, you need to:

1. Give the users exposure to the idea and slowly integrate it into their day-to-day lives and operations.

2. Facilitating proper training through sessions and process manuals can help them feel more comfortable while diving into the unknown.

3. The next stage in this cycle is crucial: gathering feedback. Understanding users' likes, dislikes, pain points, and other areas of opportunity can help strengthen their relationships and trust. From there, it's time to act.

4. After gathering feedback, you move into the optimization phase, taking the detailed information received and implementing it as part of the continuous cycle.

By utilizing this mindset, you can bring your users with you on the transformation journey through consensus and collaboration—like a dragonfly, taking processes in your department, organization, and beyond through a metamorphosis as you improve them.

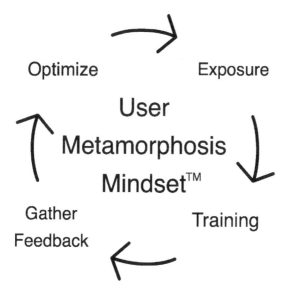

The User Metamorphosis Mindset can be applied during the Larva Stage in the Dragonfly Construct. As you identify areas of opportunity and provide solutions, bring your users along on the journey from the beginning —who knows, they may even have ideas you haven't thought about. User experience plays a crucial role in user engagement and product adoption in delivering value to customers. It refers to users' overall experience and satisfaction when interacting with a product, service, or system. In today's highly competitive market, companies recognize that providing a positive user experience is essential for attracting and retaining customers. Here are some key reasons why UX is necessary for delivering value to customers:

1. Customer Satisfaction: User experience directly impacts customer satisfaction. Customers are more likely to be satisfied with a seamless, intuitive, and enjoyable product or service experience. Positive experiences lead to happy customers, and satisfied customers are more likely to become loyal advocates for a brand, repeat their purchases, and recommend the product or service to others.

2. Increased Engagement: A well-designed user experience increases user engagement. When a product or service is intuitive, easy to use, and visually appealing, customers are likelier to engage with it for longer. Engaged users spend more time interacting with a product, exploring its features, and deriving value from it. This can lead to increased usage, higher retention rates, and a greater chance of upselling or cross-selling opportunities.

3. Competitive Advantage: User experience can be a significant differentiator in a crowded market. In many industries, products or services with similar features and functionalities compete for customers' attention. However, those who prioritize delivering a superior user experience often stand out from the competition. Companies can gain a competitive edge by providing an exceptional user experience, differentiate their offerings, and capture market share.

4. Customer Empathy: A user-centered design approach, which focuses on understanding users' needs, goals,

and pain points, helps build empathy with customers. By empathizing with their users, companies can design products and services that address real user challenges and provide meaningful solutions. This leads to better customer satisfaction and builds long-term customer relationships based on trust and loyalty.

5. Enhanced Usability: A good user experience emphasizes usability, making products and services easier to understand, learn, and navigate. When a product or service is intuitive and requires minimal effort, customers can achieve their desired outcomes more efficiently. This reduces frustration, errors, and the need for customer support, resulting in higher productivity and a smoother customer journey.

6. Brand Perception: User experience significantly influences how customers perceive a brand. A well-crafted user experience conveys a sense of professionalism, reliability, and attention to detail. Customers often associate positive experiences with the brand, leading to a positive brand image and reputation. On the other hand, a poor user experience can damage a brand's reputation and drive customers away, as negative experiences are likely to be shared through word-of-mouth and online reviews.

Simply put, user experience is vital for delivering value to customers. It fosters customer satisfaction, increases engagement, provides a competitive advantage, demonstrates empathy, enhances usability, and shapes brand perception. Companies can create long-term customer loyalty and drive growth by prioritizing UX design and consistently delivering positive user experiences.

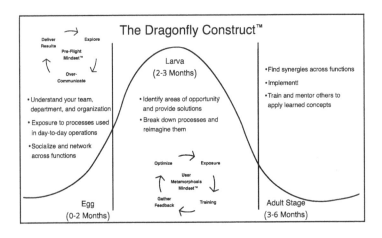

A recent example of this was with my current team. I purposely introduced a new process for an activity carried out for years by utilizing a cloud service instead of the standard on-premises offering. I saw the anguish and some trying to revert to the original process. As disruptive as this was, I stepped back and realized I had quickly forced a change without taking a phased approach or understanding viewpoints. But with that said, if we can't adapt to something new quickly, how do we expect our users to do the same?

Another personal experience using this was when I worked for a large retail telecom company; while my stint in the role was short, I achieved immense progress. I was tasked with selling a specific smartphone in a regional sales competition in partnership with the smartphone provider. Having leveraged what I learned from the video game retailer, I quickly researched the product and highlighted key elements to drive excitement and demand. I looked at each of these elements from the lens of the customer to understand the right level of exposure and training needed to get their attention and steer them away from the two most prevalent smartphone companies. As I demonstrated the capabilities and competitive advantage of the phone, which I was using as my daily driver, I took the feedback from my employees, management, and customers and began optimizing the strategy. By doing this, I sold the most in my region, won the sales competition, and was also in the top 100 in the entire company. Through solution selling, I was able to provide customers with an excellent cellphone experience based on their needs and wants, tied with the cellphone company's expansive product line and competitive edge.

The Do Better Mindset

"Do better" is a phrase that can drive people to anger or sadness. It is a critical phrase that questions the work historically done before. But what if I told you it could also drive motivation and process improvement? After creating the Dragonfly Construct, I realized that I needed to add to the holistic process and institute different mindsets to aid in driving change and improving processes.

When I started my career in retail sales working for a large video game retailer, I quickly realized I had a knack for it. I remember the first time I was number one in my store for performance metrics —I was so excited and motivated that I took it to my district manager, who immediately responded with "Do Better." At first, I thought, "What a weird response," but I continued. Months later, I was number one in my district and once again was met with "Do better." At this point, I was disappointed and confused; was the work and effort I put in not good enough? I took the feedback and continued. Finally, months later, I was number one in my region. I thought to myself, this is it – my work will finally be appreciated... but I was wrong. Once again, I was met with "Do better". I immediately challenged my district manager to understand why he kept telling me to do better, and his response shocked me and stuck with me to this day. He said, "The moment you stop trying to do better is the moment you settle and stop trying to improve the things around you." That one sentence put everything into perspective for me. From a process improvement perspective, there are always ways to do better in how we approach situations. Remember that telling someone to do better in this sense may not mean someone hasn't done well but that they can continue to improve.

After my encounter with my district manager, I applied the Do Better Mindset and adapted it over the years, even as I entered the corporate world. Around the office in my current role, I always assess the work my team is doing and often tell them to "do better." They know what I mean by that, as it's not intended to put them down but to inspire and motivate others to continue pushing past what they think can be accomplished – and sometimes, they dish it right back.

The Do Better Mindset is a process in itself of continuous improvement.

1. Starting with the identification of the process in mind, this can be anything from a small process, such as pulling a report and archiving audit evidence, to more complex processes, such as vendor onboarding and transfer-in checklists for organizations, other processes, and vendors transferring into an organization.

2. Next, seek to understand the interdependencies, meaning what processes are tied to it and how changing it impacts those, often leading to changing one process to impact many. Using vendor onboarding as an example, many processes and stakeholders are involved. Breaking down each subprocess can help identify interdependencies and the impact of changing anything else in the process. Considering what was covered during the Larva Stage, ensure that you know every other process connected to the one you are changing and provide proper notification and agreement secured before changing anything. The last thing you want is to waste time looking at enhancing a process tied to many others that could break the other ones in place.

3. When looking at vendor onboarding, you have the direct management and leadership team, sourcing, vendor management, and resource management running their processes in parallel to achieve the overall

onboarding process. You may improve the process by decreasing time spent on specific processes through re-engineering or complete removal of steps. As you look to make any changes, reach out to the right stakeholder or management team to understand and challenge the workflow to see what can be streamlined; once you get the initial buy-in, it's time to move to the next stage.

4. From there, you can get the necessary approval from your manager, stakeholders, or even parents and family members if you apply this to your daily life. Make sure to document approvals in emails so you can refer back to them for audit purposes, to cover yourself for potential legal issues, or for achievement purposes. It helps to give a small presentation for your stakeholders into the purpose of the process, process steps or flow, and what is connected to it, along with the changes you are proposing with the benefits. This will help answer any initial questions a manager may have as there is typically hesitancy or reluctance with changing processes.

5. From there, you implement the change in the process –However, now is not the time to stop.

6. Continue to revisit the process over time to assess its impact. Creating a feedback loop with the teams impacted by the process change can give you awareness of what is working or isn't.

If you run into roadblocks or problems, simply pivot and make the necessary adjustments. The beauty of processes is that you can always correct mistakes or further streamline them after implementing them. Remember, no process is final.

The Do Better Mindset can be applied during the Adult Stage in the Dragonfly Construct, pushing oneself to continue implementing change even after completing your initial goal to drive productivity and efficiency saves at work and home. After solving one problem, keep it on the back burner and assess how to improve it later.

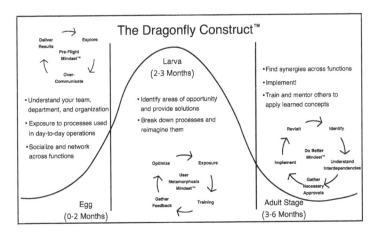

Remember, no process is final. All it takes is for someone to speak out, challenge the status quo, and push past any self-doubt or criticism from others. If you are on the fence about raising your hand to change something, remember – YOU are your most prominent critic, YOU are your biggest blocker, and YOU can set the bar for your work ethic and build your brand to go on to accomplish great things. "Do Better" is a mindset that can come across as hurtful, but through proper communication, explanation, and guidance, it's a recipe for success.

As stated previously, my team has heard it from me numerous times, allowing them to think outside the box to solve complex problems and improve our organization and ourselves. By breaking down everyday processes, you can find ways to do better by continuously improving yourself and your team. Ignore the phrase "it's always been done this way" and understand interdependencies that bridge the gap and save time.

As you read this today, keep this in mind: whether you are still in school, going off to college, entering the workforce, or ready to take the next step in your career. I challenge everyone reading this... to Do Better!

Case Study 2 – Utilizing the User Metamorphosis Mindset

Audience: Organizations (offsite activity or general team building exercise) and Individuals (personal, high school, or college class activity).

Purpose: Using Chapter 2: The Importance of a Good Mindset, select one area of opportunity (personal or work-related) and run it through the User Metamorphosis Mindset. This exercise will help challenge you to think outside the box and develop unique solutions to solve everyday problems or processes you are exposed to.

Structure: 500-1,500-word analysis

Process:

Step 1. Improvements

1. Identify an area of opportunity
2. Highlight the interdependencies (are there existing processes connected to it?)

Step 2. Execution

1. Provide a minimum of two solutions
2. Test the Applicability
   a. Run the solution(s) through the User Metamorphosis Mindset
      1. Exposure
      2. Training
      3. Gather Feedback
      4. Optimize

Step 3. Detailed Analysis

Provide a detailed write-up on the area of opportunity, potential solution(s), analysis of the User Metamorphosis Mindset, and proposed execution time.
Be sure to include the following:

1. Sample size
2. Training conducted (what idea was shared, what methods were selected)
3. Feedback received
4. What was optimized and enhanced based on feedback
5. What was/is to be implemented and the potential benefits

Step 4. Check Your Understanding

Based on your analysis, include responses to the below questions:

1. What made you decide to select the area of opportunity?
2. What was the reason for choosing the proposed solution(s)?
3. Did you receive any conflicting feedback? How did you address it? If not, how would you have handled it?
4. How can you apply the User Metamorphosis Mindset to other areas?

Case Study 3 – Operating with a Do Better Mindset

Audience: Organizations (offsite activity or general team building exercise) and Individuals (personal, high school, or college class activity).

Purpose: Using Chapter 2: The Importance of a Good Mindset, select one area of opportunity (personal or work-related) in a process that was recently updated (>= 6 months) and run it through the Do Better Mindset. This exercise will help revisit what has already been improved to identify new solutions. It will challenge you to think outside the box and develop unique solutions to solve everyday problems or processes they are exposed to.

Structure: 500-1,500-word analysis

Process:

Step 1. Improvements

1.   Identify an area of opportunity

Step 2. Execution

1.   Provide a minimum of two solutions
2.   Test the Applicability

    a.   Run the solution(s) through Do Better Mindset
1. Identify
2. Understand interdependencies
3. Gather approvals (if applicable)
4. Implement
5. Revisit (post 6+ months, if time allows)

Step 3. Detailed Analysis

Provide a detailed write-up with the area of opportunity, potential solution(s), analysis of the Do Better Mindset, and proposed execution time.

Be sure to include the following:

1. Identified area of opportunity and proposed solution(s)
2. Share any interdependencies that exist and what teams are involved
3. What approvals were required before implementation?
4. What is the proposed time to implement?
5. Revisit (post 6+ months, if time allows)
    a.   After implementing the change, reflect

on it after 6 months to track the impact
and benefits of your changes
b.   Does anything need to be enhanced?
c.   Are there any new issues that came to
light after implementing your solution(s)?

Step 4. Check Your Understanding

Based on your analysis, include responses to the below
questions:

1.   When was the last time the process you selected
was updated?
2.   What made you decide to select the area of
opportunity?
3.   What was the reason for choosing the proposed
solution(s)?
4.   How do you think you can apply the Do Better
Mindset to other areas?

CHAPTER 3

Integrating the Dragonfly Construct

When looking at what makes a company successful, aside from profits, are the employees. Something as simple as stating that the employees are the company is often overlooked. It is a clear, basic concept. If you want your company to do well, you should put all your efforts into caring for your employees. Creating a healthy work environment allows your employees to fully engage in projects and everyday job activities, improving processes and solution thinking. Keeping your employees happy creates maximum output, leading to low absenteeism. If you are facing problems pertaining to absenteeism, take a step back, analyze why, and try to take control of it. When you invest in your employees, it shows that you care. Take time out of your day to speak with them one-on-one. Doing so lets you figure out what might be causing problems in their work and understand their viewpoints on how things can be done better.

"It's My Castle" Mentality

When I worked for a large video game retailer, there was one thing that I instantly noticed. They often treated their corporate employees better than the frontline workers. There needed to be uniformity in the training or development process. Many retail managers had the "It's my castle" mentality management style. This is when one creates all the rules and reigns over their store or department with a tight grip. They tend to ignore policies and procedures and train their employees how they want to, not necessarily how the company wants them to. They also look out for themselves with the decisions they make. I've had several conversations where I was told that we were not promoting someone solely because they did well in their current position, and they did not want to replace them. After talking with that associate, it was clear that they had been trying to move up but saw no progress. By not having a selfish mindset and only thinking about hitting comps or bonuses, you can set up different tracks for each employee to help them attain their goals. While someone is excellent in a position, allowing them to move up in the same corporation will allow them to utilize their skills on a grand scale and, in return, bring more profit to the company.

Once promoted into any position with power, it's not uncommon for people to want to take complete control. When describing this situation, the word power trip comes to mind. Those with little management experience or reluctance to lead will try to tell themselves they are better than their peers. They tie success to making money rather than focusing on the well-being of their employees. Your employees will instantly notice when you start putting other things ahead of them, creating workplace hostility. The moment they feel mistreated or undervalued is when they will look elsewhere for other opportunities. Whether you are the manager or employee, you can leverage the Dragonfly Construct. As a manager, run your current department holistically through the Dragonfly Construct. Remember, you are there to learn from the team as much as they are there to learn from you. By building relationships and understanding processes used in day-to-day operations, you can identify areas of opportunity and solutions. These can even be applied from a human resources perspective, focusing on your employees' well-being and improving your interactions with them. It may feel like all hope is lost as an employee, but the Dragonfly Construct can be implemented to demonstrate they are ready for more than your current position. Integrating the key concepts can establish credibility to build your brand. If it doesn't catch the attention of your direct manager, it will be noticed by those above and around them.

Addressing Turnover

Amidst "The Great Resignation," keeping employees in their roles is challenging. This is due to many factors, such as people figuring out new methods to generate cash flow outside of the standard Monday through Friday job, seeking better opportunities with flexible work schedules and more of a work-life balance, and sometimes simply poor management. Turnover, or the rate at which employees leave the workforce and are replaced, can leave managers without proper coverage and support. With that said, turnover is an everyday experience in the workforce. However, when many people go at once, it can cause problems.

When employees enter a company, they can be put into two categories: core and stepping stones, and this applies to all industries. Your core employees are eager to advance within the company, understand the role, and often go above and beyond to demonstrate their capabilities for promotion. They can also be complacent and not want to move up but get the job done; it's a vast, all-encompassing net. On the other hand, stepping stones are employees trying to gain the skills necessary for a higher position elsewhere and are prevalent in the tech industry. This is generally the group that contributes the most to turnover. Many stepping stones can become core based on how they are treated by you (the manager), other management, and the overall company. Whether your business promotes process improvement, you should teach them everything essential to help them grow themselves, your business, and future businesses. Too often, managers teach their employees the bare minimum so they do not have the skills to move up or that no company will hire them. Once these employees figure out what is happening, they feel unappreciated and quit. Integrating the Dragonfly Construct into their day-to-day lives and operations can help revitalize and motivate employees to explore new areas and solve everyday problems. Reducing turnover not only makes you look good but also makes your manager look better. It's also great when talking to stakeholders to get support for a new idea. Showing them that you can control your workplace does wonders.

I had an employee who wanted to leave and felt that they had learned everything they could in the role and wanted to explore opportunities outside of the team, stating that it wasn't about the money but learning something new and taking on a new challenge. While I am a huge proponent of developing people to succeed and take on new roles or leadership roles in and out of my team, I didn't want to lose them because of the value and strategic thinking they brought to the team. I pulled them into a room and asked what they wanted to do, what they were passionate about, and, ultimately, the role they wanted to have. The entire time, I was taking notes. By the end of the conversation, I had drafted a rough job description and informed them that it was theirs for the taking. If they could stick it out for a year, I said they would quickly gain the necessary knowledge and skill sets to enter their desired role. By integrating the job elements of their end-state, I could retain them and light a new motivational flame in them. I took the ideology of the Dragonfly Construct and modified portions of it to fit the human resources aspect. It's not a static construct and can be utilized in a myriad of ways to challenge the status quo and think outside the box to solve complex problems in any situation. While I wasn't trying to improve a process, I shifted the scope to improve the well-being and career of my employees.

The egg stage included understanding my team, department, and organization to see where I could create new opportunities for my team. The larva stage included the identification of an area of opportunity, keeping my employees on the team and happy, and the solution, creating a brand-new role based on their passions and future role in mind. Finally, the adult stage encompassed finding synergies across my organization to understand where we had gaps that could be filled based on what my employees wanted to do and implementing it. I only asked if they would do the same for their employees when they became managers. Opportunities are sometimes hard to come by, but anything is possible with the right manager and leadership.

Change Management

Change management, a framework for managing change related to people and the planning and implementation of changes in a company, is essential to ensure decisions made are seen through the lens of the employees and clients. Often seen paired with organizational behavior, or how individuals and teams interact within a company and how the interactions, both horizontally and laterally, affect a company's performance and goals. Implementing a new process function, hiring or promoting a new leader, or even consolidating or removing teams can positively or negatively impact employees. Sometimes, changes must be made against employees' wishes due to time constraints, strategy, and emerging risks, but is there a better way to tackle these situations?

The Dragonfly Construct can play a crucial role in allowing those in leadership to assess the potential impact a change may have on employees. Rather than an area of improvement relating to a process in the Larva Stage, it can be viewed as what can be done for the employees given the changes to be implemented, followed by solutions. From my experience, when significant changes are made at companies, little is done to ease employees' nerves outside of a town hall meeting – but it's time to change how things are done. As companies shift toward the Adult Stage, before or after implementation, leadership can identify synergies between two teams and provide a project that can be worked on together, driving collaboration and growth as the new team forms.

The Dragonfly Construct channels change management and process improvement, encouraging managers to think outside the box and challenge the status quo when implementing changes related to people, processes, or technology.

Productivity, Efficiency Saves, And Bears... Oh My!

Many people dislike meeting productivity goals as it challenges them to identify areas of spending to cut and strains the motivation of their employees. This can mean anything from utilizing resources more efficiently and pausing net-new headcount to layoffs. While these tasks are never easy, they are all part of doing business. However, one of the positive aspects of productivity saves is that you can improve processes and take a new look at how things are done across all aspects of a manager's role. Immediately after learning about productivity goals, the first place you should analyze is your profit and loss (P&L) charts. Look to see if there is any area you can cut back on, such as your lights being left on at night in unnecessary places. Can you cut costs around unnecessary or excessive spending? Can you strategically reinvest what you have to drive innovation across multiple functions or teams? OR can you increase in an area, such as driving additional sales to help subsidize the cuts? Can you improve a process integrated into several teams? Now, if you're working in a cost center or an area in a company that does not generate revenue, it may be challenging, but not impossible, to find ways to drive efficiency saves. At the end of the day, if you can't derive an impactful solution, it may, unfortunately, end with a reduction in headcount. If they aren't performing well (because we all know life happens) or were randomly selected as part of the layoffs, try to get an extension to revive their career. Most employee layoffs are due to not performing well as a company, low sales, etc., but if you can find a way for the employee to enhance business and increase sales, it's worth fighting for. You can leverage the Dragonfly Construct's Larva Stage to identify opportunities and solutions to save your employees. While this may not always work out as intended, it's worth a shot. If your company is outsourcing a department to a vendor, help your loyal employees to try and get them a new position within the company, and if that's not possible – get them onboarded to the vendor. This will preserve the institutional knowledge and allow them to return as full-time employees.

At some point in your career, you will endure a lousy boss who has squandered opportunities and created personal angst. Some executives and senior leaders rarely tout their festering behavior and poor decision-making. These same executives run amok, showcasing their good deeds and sizzle while being excessively entitled to admiration for such accomplishments.

Jonathan was required to purchase large equipment, technology, supplies, and other IT-related services for a mid-sized company. They did not have a purchasing manager, so he had full reign to make whatever purchases he needed for his department. These purchases were made through vendors that Jonathan had vetted and hand-selected himself. Jonathan became very close with these vendors, who supplied hundreds of thousands of dollars worth of equipment and infrastructure every quarter. Jonathan's sense of loyalty was something these suppliers valued.

The benefits of positive supplier relationships are strategically critical to a company's success. Sometimes, this loyalty can backfire if prioritized over what's best for the company. Jonathan's commitment and dedication to his suppliers had become intense. When Jonathan was tasked by his leadership to make cuts, he steered clear of making cuts to his suppliers. These vendors had become loyal to Jonathan to the point where he protected them from these cuts.

His company started to hemorrhage money, and Jonathan was cutting staff and other critical areas—instead of cutting back on his suppliers—undermining the proper function of business operations. Sometimes, loyalty can be seen as a treasured characteristic and power mode. Still, suppose this loyalty is affecting the survival of his company. In that case,

Jonathan should have gone to those vendors to work out a win-win scenario to make immediate and necessary cuts without hindering the positive relationship he had built with these vendors. Jonathan was treating these suppliers as partners, not just vendors. He was fully aware of their needs and concerns and was scared to approach them with significant changes that would affect the relevant progress of their relationship. Was Jonathan correct in standing up and protecting the relationships he had built over time and being loyal to them no matter what? Or was he in the wrong for leveraging his loyalty towards these vendors and putting the company he worked for at risk? The answer to this is for another book. Still, in this case, Jonathan should have gone to these vendors and shared with them what was happening and that he needed each one of these vendors to meet him in the middle or work out a reduction to help the bottom line that the company needed to make through financial cuts.

In some cases, issues like these arise because these leaders and decision-makers are not adequately trained or lack the experience to best execute this process. In other cases, their loyalty gets in the way, blurring the lines of best practices and encroaching on unintended negative side effects that affect decision-making.

Ultimately, Jonathan did connect with each vendor individually to work out a plan to reduce high costs, but he did so after his loyalty decisions had negatively affected the company financially.

When starting my career at a leading financial institution as an assistant vice president, I worked in a cost center and knew I had to find a way to contribute to cost saves to aid in our productivity goal. At the time, I identified a gap in the length of time it took for our contracts to be drafted, negotiated, and signed - this was due to the sheer number of contracts and the number of sourcing and legal employees. I picked up an existing contract and began to read it and learn the lingo, how the commercials were calculated, and the deal's architecture. I then took a contract coming up for renewal and began to draft the amendment. When negotiating contracts, it's important to remain at the current rate or, better yet, spend less. I took the draft to my sourcing and legal colleagues and presented them with the document. They were stunned. One of the legal employees, a senior vice president, stated that he had never seen someone from the business take a stab at drafting an amendment or a contract in his years of working at multiple companies. They agreed to allow me to write and negotiate as long as they reviewed everything prior and made the necessary adjustments. It saved time and allowed me to lessen the time to sign a contract, resulting in efficiency and cost savings. From there, I began to write and negotiate, and when I took on the 221 vendors as a vice president, it was time to execute and deliver.

By the end of my time in the role, as I was transitioning to a new position at the largest investment bank in the world, I had saved my then-company approximately $996,000. Over three years, I integrated new sub-functions into my team that included contract writing & negotiating, process improvement, resource, financial, and project management, which all aided in productivity and cost saves. Processes come in many shapes and sizes and carry different weights of importance. Taking a step out of your comfort zone and trying to solve a problem can yield great results and aid in building your brand. Remember, even if you pitch a process improvement or new idea to a manager, and they say no, it's all right. It still gets you in the process improvement mindset.

Customers Are Powerful

Above all, users and stakeholders are human. They immediately realize when a product needs to improve or is riddled with issues. As much as we may not like it, we need to give them the VIP treatment, regardless of whether the product is being used in-house or externally. From an in-house perspective, if you own a product or support one, you must ensure that you and your team listen to your users' and stakeholders' complaints and issues. Your product may be the only one available, and they have no choice but to use it; however, listening to them is a great way to show that you are engaged in bettering the product. From an external perspective, you are at the mercy of every release to ensure the product doesn't go down or that the enhancements made are actually what your users want.

My dad worked for an organization that was increasing and expanding into electronic prep materials that enabled students to practice with official test content and authentic test questions. The dive into digital test prep opportunities was a game-changer for this organization, and students were looking to master their knowledge and skills as they prepared to take the official tests. Online digital technology was new in this realm, where the CD-ROM had previously been the champion tool for this process. As these test prep tools and resources came online, the user experience and interface became problematic initially because different browsers would render material differently.

The year was 1999, the cusp of the new millennium, where online technology was the up-and-coming shiny toy, revolutionizing the Internet. The browser war between Netscape and Microsoft's Internet Explorer was full-blown in effect during this time. These browsers rendered content differently, so coding pages and test prep platforms became somewhat of a nightmare. My dad worked with a fantastic team of developers and testers, and he was tasked to work on the front-end user interface and experience of these online test prep tools.

As this organization grew and expanded, so did its online services. Growth was good. It meant that the organization exceeded expectations and provided an important service that thousands of students readily purchased. As my father shared stories of his time at this organization, he remembered how he had become the bottleneck. Several programmers and quality assurance individuals were testing out bugs, but only one developer was in charge of the front-end user experience— my father. There were days when he was working nights and weekends, sixty to eighty hours a week, trying to keep up with the demands of his role. He loved doing the work, so he never complained, but his work was never well appreciated either because all they could see was the bottleneck delaying the release of these prep tools and services.

When management is more focused on deadlines instead of providing the necessary help and staffing to accomplish such exponential tasks and provide for the well-being and health of its employees, it tends to lead to poor work performance, fatigue, heightened employee emotions, stress, and ultimately, burnout. Not once did HR or his boss approach him about his health and well-being. All he received from them was reprimands for falling behind on tasks and deadlines.

Sometimes, improvements or growth of new products and services sound excellent on paper. Still, if leadership doesn't pay attention to the needs and health of the employees to avoid burnout, it creates a demoralizing culture to the detriment of their work and ultimately can impact the customer.

Word-of-mouth is also a powerful tool that a user or customer possesses. It can build up a business or tear it down. A thousand great experiences can all be undone by one bad interaction. Take customer interactions seriously with your team and develop them to bring out the best in them and everyone who walks through your doors or interacts with them via phone. While you can't make everyone happy, be sure to leverage the User Metamorphosis Mindset in both situations to ensure that users and stakeholders are heard and that the optimal strategy can be utilized while sprint planning and selecting what enhancements or bugs need to be addressed promptly to keep your product competitive.

During my time at the world's largest investment bank, I led a team of product managers to enhance a vendor-owned product used for vendor onboarding. After assessing the full capability of the product, I saw an opportunity to improve a specific feature to integrate our data and give users a one-stop shop to perform their day-to-day operations. Believe it or not, there was resistance. Many were used to the process over the years, and even though it required less time, it was something new. I'm sure many product managers know the feeling I had when I learned that the business was against it. However, as I stated in the Preface, as our regulatory and technology landscapes adapt, so should we. I made the change in parallel while keeping the existing process in place and slowly exposed the users to the new process. With proper training, I could demonstrate the need for the change and highlight new features that could be utilized on the specific tab. Over the month, I integrated their feedback into the product and began optimizing. When it was completed, the business shifted from the old process and adopted the new one. The company was big on driving consensus; initially, I was not too fond of it. I was used to implementing what was needed and making life easier for the end user. However, over time, I grew to learn the importance of it. As a product manager, it's more important to listen to your users and ultimately give them what's needed (to a certain extent). When dealing with users, it's important not to rush or make rash decisions that could torment them and steer them further from susceptibility to change. While not all situations are the same, and users may not always agree to adopt a new process, doing your best to drive change and innovate what "has always been done that way" opens the door and receptiveness to new changes in the future. Not everyone will like the changes made, but as long as your stakeholders are happy, it's essential to ensure you drive the company forward.

A Recap On Integrating The Dragonfly Construct

Like the dragonfly, the Dragonfly Construct is easily adaptable to any situation. Stepping out of your comfort zone can be scary, but if a dragonfly can survive its egg stage amongst the perils it faces in its environment to grow into a beautiful insect and provide for the world around it, so can you. Many of us have had ideas to improve something yet never brought it to fruition. This can be due to a lack of management support, being uncomfortable with raising your hand, or fear. These are all common things, mainly being uncomfortable and fearful. Pushing past these can seem daunting, but sharing ideas drives innovation. As you listen to conversations around you, pick up on key topics such as pain points, performance, and the organization's direction. Find a way to include yourself in the conversation and make the introduction. This will help you network, meet various people, and give you the platform to solve their problems. By leveraging the Dragonfly Construct, you can lessen the time in the stages while still having an impact.

Whether you are dealing with an "it's my castle" manager,

addressing turnover, overseeing change management, tackling productivity and efficiency saves, or are responsible for products, the scenarios are endless when using the Dragonfly Construct.

Using the Dragonfly Construct Outside of Work

The Dragonfly Construct would not be a dynamic process improvement methodology if you couldn't apply it to the world around you. By breaking down each stage and applying it to your daily life, you can visualize your routines as processes and see how to alter them to achieve your goals. Typically, at the beginning of every year, we devise New Year's resolutions (although many quit after a month) to better our lives and accomplish something meaningful. To do this, pick one routine you think you can improve, decreasing time spent or enhancing your work.

Grab a piece of paper and run the routine through the Dragonfly Construct, now with minor tweaks compared to using it for business. Note that some routines and habits may take less than six months to break or remove; it is recommended that you spend at least 30 days going through the process at a minimum. This can be applied to something as simple as your morning routine to something more complex, such as quitting caffeine or smoking. While results may not be guaranteed in some cases, as the Dragonfly Construct is simply a methodology that can be used to solve problems, if you are struggling with something more profound, please seek the necessary medical attention and communicate with your friends, family, spouses, partners, or coworkers. From a personal perspective, it allows you to organize your areas of opportunity and provide solutions to enhance routines or habits.

The Egg Stage

At this stage, you should already know about yourself: strengths, weaknesses, passions, etc., and this gives you the advantage over the existing routines or processes used in your "day-to-day" operations. However, you have already introduced habits that may be harder to break into your life. Having an accountability partner, whether a spouse, partner, family member, or friend, will help immensely as you begin your journey —this runs in parallel with 'socializing and networking across functions'. Socializing your goal and networking with others forms a partnership between you and the person or group of people. Depending on the routine or habit, remember, it's okay to be vulnerable when asking for help.

The Pre-Flight Mindset

Yes, even the mindsets can be applied in your personal life to aid you on your journey. Before thinking about your areas of opportunity or solutions, use the Pre-Flight Mindset to explore yourself, over-communicate your intentions with friends, family, or coworkers, and deliver results by taking initial feedback and establishing accountability partners.

A recent habit I adjusted was my love (or addiction) for caffeine. I took a step back and realized that I was consuming too much caffeine throughout the day, which impacted my health in multiple ways – and added up financially over the years. I would have a coffee in the morning and one to two energy drinks (if you know me well enough, you know which one) throughout the day. I knew I needed to adjust my routine, which had become a habit. I explored my options, over-communicated with my friends and coworkers (synonymous), and began to take their feedback and look at potential opportunities.

The Larva Stage

When entering the larva stage, leveraging your accountability partners, or simply tackling it on your own, you can begin to identify your areas of opportunity and potential solutions. Sometimes, it helps to break down your routine(s) by writing out the steps you take to see where you can cut or altogether remove it and providing solutions or recommendations.

The User Metamorphosis Mindset

Using the User Metamorphosis Mindset typically enhances user or product experiences, but it can also be used in your journey toward altering or breaking a routine or habit. As you've already identified your accountability partners, give them exposure to your areas of opportunity and solutions on how you'll address them. The training step can be used to research alternate methods or watch videos on people who have done something similar – even surveying your friends, family, or coworkers. From there, gather feedback from your account-ability partner(s) to ensure it meets your intended purpose and move towards optimizing how you'll implement it.

Continuing with the example of my caffeine habit, I used the User Metamorphosis Mindset to give exposure to my areas of opportunity and solutions. The main one was to cut out coffee entirely and reassess from there initially. I researched alternate methods to reduce drinking coffee, as I wasn't quite ready to give up energy drinks. As silly as this might sound, I was determined to cut down on my caffeine habit, so I gathered some feedback from my coworkers and put my implementation plan together to optimize this one of many routines in my life.

The Adult Stage

Finding synergies when breaking habits or changing routines is easier than you think. Chances are your friends or family have similar habits or routines and may have cut them out of their lives or found better ways to do them. At this stage, it's time to act and implement those solutions against your areas of opportunity. It is often easier said than done, as a routine can become a habit, and it takes 30 days to break it on average. But by leveraging the stages of the Dragonfly Construct, you can do your best to change how you operate and improve the processes in your day-to-day life. From there, you can take what you've learned and help others to take similar steps to impact their lives positively.

The Do Better Mindset

Once you've completed your goal of reducing time spent or completely removing a routine or habit from your life, it's time to review and see if it can be further enhanced or done better. Identify the routine or habit you recently changed (nothing less than three months after) and understand if there are any existing or new interdependencies attached to it. Begin to map out your areas of opportunity and solutions. The 'Gather Necessary Approvals' step can be repurposed to mean checking with your accountability partners before you make any adjustments, depending on the routine or habit – ultimately, it is your call at the end of the day. From there, you implement the process again, continuing to revisit it every three months or until you are satisfied with the result.

Finally, I implemented the change and removed coffee from my morning routine. Things were going well until I realized that my interdependency was tied to my sugar intake, another habit I need to adjust at some point. I consulted with some coworkers on alternatives and was suggested a strawberry acai refresher from the "Siren" company. While it had caffeine, it was significantly lower compared to the coffee I was drinking before. I even downsized from a venti to a grande.

I implemented the new change, but after revisiting it, I realized that I was still consuming an additional two energy drinks containing ample amounts of caffeine and sugar. I reviewed my routine and removed one of the energy drinks while only consuming it three times a week (a 70% reduction!). While the change in the process didn't completely cut out my caffeine intake, it lessened it and introduced fruits into my morning routine via the refresher (hey, it's a start). The beauty of process improvement is that it's never final, and there are always ways to do better.

CHAPTER 4

Other Uses for the Dragonfly Construct

Building Your Brand

What makes a brand, and how can it apply to you? Several self-help books and articles exist on this, but I think it's important to mention it in this book as the mindsets and overarching Dragonfly Construct can aid in propelling you forward. A company's brand signifies to customers its purpose and markets the benefits of using it versus its competitors. Toyota and Honda come to mind when you think of reliability, safety, and good resale value for cars. Aside from their annual or seasonal sales commercials, they have built their brand by letting their product line speak for themselves. In addition, word-of-mouth and the passing of cars from generation to generation continue to build the brand; this is also prevalent in Subaru commercials. Many may not realize that they can take that same mindset and apply it to themselves. A brand is built on reputation and how others perceive you. When someone mentions your name, what comes to mind? Is it that you are a hard worker who delivers results, or are you unreliable and late? These things are crafted when you start a job or new role.

Leveraging the mindsets in this chapter during the stages of the Dragonfly Construct will allow you to gain credibility, respect, and ultimately formalize your brand and what you stand for. Once you've established yourself, it's not a one-and-done ordeal. You need to continue to assess where you stand in the eyes of your peers, colleagues, and management and adapt accordingly to fix any negative perceptions. Mistakes happen, and it's okay to fail, but at the end of the day, your brand matters and will help you progress in your career.

Time Management

You may be wondering what the Dragonfly Construct has to do with time management, but it integrates well within it. Whether you are changing processes at work or in your personal life, other things can get in the way. We often take on large workloads, voluntarily or not, which forces us to balance our time accordingly, sometimes bleeding into our personal lives.

The concept of a work-life balance is often thought of as a 50-50 split between work and personal life; however, in my opinion, it's subjective. I'm sure you've seen the picture of the triangle that says "Work, Life, and Sleep: You Can Only Pick Two." But what if I told you you can do all three or more?

Time management, or how you organize, plan, and divide the amount of time to dedicate to work, school, social, sleep, and hobbies, forces creativity as we only have 24 hours in a day. By taking a step back, you can organize your day into a Gantt chart or simple checklist with target "due dates" for what you want to accomplish for the day. If you are focusing on your career or school, you may prioritize more time on those areas, and sometimes other areas may suffer, but it's always temporary. I often sacrificed time with family and friends, missing birthday parties and reunions, which led me to develop a standard for myself in how I operate. I mentioned earlier that a 50-50 split is subjective, and that's because there is more to life than work and home. By pushing yourself, you can achieve great things and make a difference. If the standard viewpoint on a work-life balance suits you better, adhere to that. There is no right or wrong way to plan your day.

With the Dragonfly Construct, you can apply all the mindsets when planning your day. The Pre-Flight mindset allows you to explore what needs to be done, over-communicate your plan, and deliver results through accomplishing your tasks.

The User Metamorphosis mindset allows you to give exposure to your work to those around you for input. Training your users also will enable you to learn while on the job or when completing tasks. It's always good to get feedback along the way. Some may say you're doing too much, but trust me, it can be done. Finally, optimize how you deliver projects and personal tasks for others and yourself.

In the Do Better mindset, you can apply the concepts to identify what is and isn't working, understand interdependencies with your tasks to optimize further the work being done, implement the changes, and continue to revisit them for maximum efficiency.

For me, time management has been a skill that I've developed over the years. I've been working full-time since 10th grade, allowing me to hone this skill set and set the foundation for juggling upwards of nine activities simultaneously. When I completed my doctorate and prior degrees, I worked, on average, 70 hours a week and balanced my relationship and other priorities. At each step of my journey, I was told by friends and family that it wasn't sustainable and that I couldn't handle it – it then became a mission to prove them wrong. Fast forward to today. I work as a senior vice president for one of the largest financial institutions in the world but also manage Evolve Like a Dragonfly LLC and the Neopte Foundation, Inc. as the President and Chief Executive Officer, all while having a successful marriage.

Everything is possible if you put your mind to it. Pushing past the doubters and your thoughts, you can achieve anything. It may involve sacrifices but know it's temporary. Mike Rowe says, "Work ethic is important, because, unlike intelligence, athleticism, charisma, or any other natural attribute, it's a choice". Building your brand and optimizing your life through time management through the Dragonfly Construct gives new perspectives to you and those around you. Remember, whether you know it or not, your journey inspires and motivates those around you.

Personal Injuries

This one is interesting as I initially didn't think about how the Dragonfly Construct could be used when dealing with personal injuries. My grandma reached out to me one morning, and right after waking up, she immediately ran her shoulder injury through the Dragonfly Construct. When dealing with a shoulder injury or similar injury, you may struggle with how to get around and adapt your lifestyle while awaiting the healing process to finalize. As you enter the Egg Stage, you begin to understand the limits of your injury and gain additional exposure to your day-to-day routine and the tasks you usually perform. In the Larva Stage, you identify opportunities to perform your everyday tasks, considering your current situation while breaking down the processes to imagine new ways of doing things. Finally, in the Adult Stage, you can find synergies with how you go about your day and conduct your routines given your injury. You slowly start to implement the changes and take into account the progress you make. If it doesn't work, scale back and reimagine how you tackle the different situations. Once you get it down, you can go about your day in a somewhat typical fashion and share your tips and processes with those with similar injuries. By no means does the Dragonfly Construct constitute a cure for personal injuries, but it allows you to think outside the box with how you operate when dealing with one.

With the Dragonfly Construct, the opportunities to grow and expand the world around you are limitless. While only three areas were mentioned in this section, look around to see how you can best apply the Dragonfly Construct at work or home. By using all or some of the concepts and mindsets for everyday problems or scenarios, you can find new ways to accomplish your goals, routines, or general tasks.

CHAPTER 5

The Dragonfly Construct Framework

After creating the Dragonfly Construct, I realized it catered to managers and employees. It left out a target demographic, companies. It needed to be adaptable if I wanted to roll out a truly dynamic methodology and construct. The purpose of the Dragonfly Construct Framework is to allow companies to implement it as part of their core frameworks to drive change, new opportunities, and process improvements. The framework provides a new approach to problem-solving and process improvement. When looking at the structure of an organization, the Dragonfly Construct Framework sits right above it. The ideologies should permeate the spans and layers, extending laterally and horizontally. If done successfully, you will see a culture shift to be more process improvement-minded, creating out-of-the-box thinkers and rewarding innovation that stems from it.

While the Dragonfly Construct can tremendously impact an individual and their environment, a proper framework must be established for this to be applied across an entire company. The Dragonfly Construct Framework brings together four unique objectives to aid in a company's advancement of processes. This framework builds the foundation for process improvement across an organization using four core objectives: DCF.1 Optimization & Productivity, DCF.2 Client Centricity, DCF.3 Compliance & Controls, and DCF.4 Innovation. These were developed over my years in the Risk & Governance space and tested individually and as a group to understand the correlation and relevance to process improvement; however, they can be applied in any field. Each sub-objective (notated as DCF.XXX) can utilize the Dragonfly Construct to create or re-engineer an existing process.

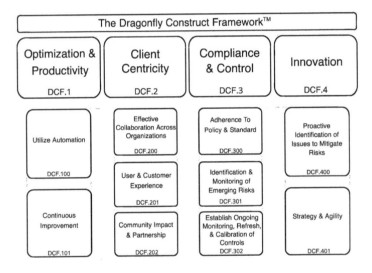

DCF.1 Optimization & Productivity

Optimization, or the ability to make something more efficient, coupled with productivity, the ability to maximize input for greater output, is vital to a company. Optimization utilizes automation and continuous improvement to drive process improvement and efficiency. When you optimize a process, you can dissect it to understand the end-to-end flow and determine what steps may be redundant or unnecessary or where you can add something to reduce the time spent. Productivity is typically associated with meeting a financial reduction goal by the end of a set period, often a year. Like optimization, productivity also benefits from automation and continuous improvement. Productivity can be broken down into two buckets: direct cost saves and efficiency saves. Efficiency saves focus on reducing time spent on a process multiplied by the number of times it's performed over a year to determine the total number of hours a year saved and where and how that time is reinvested.

DCF.100 Utilize Automation

Automation is the key to driving optimization and productivity. With the rise of artificial intelligence and machine learning (AI/ML), there are more opportunities to drive automation in everyday processes, decrease time spent on manual processes, and allow focus on more critical tasks and projects. While some fear that automation will put them out of a job, it's important to note that while automation relieves tedious, menial tasks, it still needs to be managed, monitored, and improved, which requires a physical person to act. The Automation Model can help provide a structured guide for driving automation.

1. Identify the process to be automated. This can be done by analyzing the current processes and selecting one that uses a rules-based approach, utilizing if statements (if X = Y, Then Z).

2. Understand and assess the technical capabilities. This is not just from an AI/ML standpoint but also from your engineering team's current book of work and other conflicting priorities.

3. Once an agreement is made, then development starts. This may take time and can sometimes identify blockers, but show support and appreciation to the engineers.

4. It must be tested in a user acceptance testing (UAT) environment. This will allow you to find any kinks in the automation and test the functionality while documenting the work done for audit purposes.

5. From there, it's time to promote it in the production environment and continue monitoring it. If the automation fails, roll it back and partner with your engineering team to assess the path forward.

DCF.1 OPTIMIZATION & PRODUCTIVITY				
AUTOMATION MODEL				
IDENTIFY	ASSESS TECHNICAL CAPABILITIES	DEVELOP	TEST	PROMOTE

Automation. A word that scares many as it is associated with job reductions and driving redundancy in roles. However, there are many positives to leveraging automation to drive companies forward. I recently read a Forbes article by Timo Elliott on 'The Power Of Artificial Intelligence Vs. The Power Of Human Intelligence' highlighted the importance that AI plays in our world, citing in 2021 that AI augmentation would have created > $2.8 trillion of business value and save 6.2 billion man-hours globally (a study conducted by Gartner). Timo mentions that AI will boost opportunities and unleash the full power of human intelligence. That sentence stood out to me as many forget that behind AI are people and teams who manage the backend, strengthening human skills like leadership and creativity. AI may introduce automation into tedious day-to-day activities, but we must develop the ideas and how they scale. It's time to dare to dream big about how we can optimize the world around us.

DCF.101 Continuous Improvement

Continuous improvement, or the ongoing effort to improve products, services, and processes, is critical to ensuring they don't go stale. As users and clients shift priorities and price elasticity increases, it's important to check that the products, services, and processes are up to par. The beauty of continuous improvement is that it never stops. Managers, employees, and companies should always review what currently exists and imagine the next iteration and how to get there. The Continuous Improvement Model focuses on:

1. Identifying the product, service, or process to be improved.

2. Utilize the Do Better mindset to understand interdependencies, gather approvals, implement, and revisit what was done to ensure they are meeting the needs of your company, users, and clients.

3. Monitor the progress and capture any necessary feedback for future improvements and enhancements.

DCF.2 Client Centricity

Client centricity, or understanding a client's situations, perceptions, and expectations, is essential no matter what industry you work in. Clients, or customers, are at the center of every company as they generate revenue, drive up stock prices, and bring about additional clients. Companies establish customer service departments to assist and support clients with issues tied to their products or services. These departments measure their client centricity through a net promoter score. But what happens if you don't work in a customer service department and don't have a net promoter score?

DCF.200 Effective Collaboration Across Organizations

Client centricity can be accomplished through effective collaboration across organizations. This means working together towards a common goal of delivering a best-in-class service to a client. Companies may operate in silos, often not communicating fully or at all with their peers or outside their departments. This can prove fatal to addressing the needs of a client. This is the challenging part; however, as part of the Egg Stage of the Dragonfly Construct, managers and employees should not only understand their team, department, and organization but socialize and network across functions. This is important to better understand what teams are working on and the challenges they are facing.

Whether you are a project or product manager, a people manager, or an individual contributor, you can lead the charge to break down silos and connect people through effective collaboration. Who knows, you may be able to bridge the gap and assist in solving a longstanding problem.

DCF.201 User & Customer Experience

The impact an upset user or client can have on a company is a massive reminder that customers are powerful. Proper planning, feedback, and training are needed when companies seek to roll out a new product, feature, or enhancement. The User Metamorphosis mindset can be utilized as part of the Larva Stage to ensure the right level of exposure, training, feedback, and optimization are covered before going live. This will help strengthen the relationship and trust between users and clients to deliver an optimal product or service experience.

DCF.202 Community Impact & Partnership

The impact a company can have on the community is crucial. Companies can leverage the Dragonfly Construct to solve problems in the community and give back through volunteer events and donations, as well as by providing both high-school and college-level apprenticeships. By engaging and identifying the areas of opportunity in the local community, you can set a precedent for how companies and communities should inter-act. Not only does the company provide jobs, which increases spending power, but it also can give opportunities to those who want to make a difference. The culture at a company should encourage employees to go out and make a difference in their community so they feel appreciated, which can yield long-lasting results that mutually benefit all parties.

My dad recently told me about how he opened a business bank account with a new bank. Within weeks, they received an invitation in the mail with free tickets to a musical at his local theater. It was a thank-you gift for being a client. He stated, "It was a beautiful experience to get invited to some-thing cool. We got to dress up and attend. When we got there, not only were there other clients invited to this event, but their bank employees too. It was the bank's way of appreciat-ing both their staff and clients. It may have been expensive on their end, but it was completely worth the effort. We and others walked away from the experience not only feeling great and proud of the bank that we had just joined but also felt appreciated in a way that no other bank had ever done for us in the past."

When organizations invest in their teams and their clients, it pays dividends in the long run. The other piece of the community outreach was that the bank didn't just pay for everyone's tickets to attend the musical, they also partnered with the theater at a community level by sponsoring the musical and other community events. The bank truly wanted to make a difference in the community, and they indeed made it happen.

DCF.3 Compliance & Controls

Compliance and controls are essential in the work environment, as most processes have controls tied to them. A control is a measurement of the effectiveness of a process with the company's risk appetite or the level of risk deemed acceptable. These are often paired with Key Performance Indicators (KPIs), which measure the performance of a control, and Key Risk Indicators (KRIs), which measure the risk of a control. An example of a company-wide control is whether all employees completed their corporate-required training. When implementing a process, you want to ensure that you can measure its success and highlight any risks that may be present through a control or set of controls. The other aspect to consider is adherence to compliance. Every country has its own set of regulators that produce different laws, rules, and regulations that must be followed, with high-level laws making up company policies and procedures.

DCF.300 Adherence to Policy & Standards

At the heart of every process is an overarching policy and standards. As discussed in the Adult Stage of the Dragonfly

Construct, it's important to understand the interdependencies tied to a process. This can be expanded to understanding the key policies and standards that lay the foundation for the process, along with any laws, rules, or regulations. Failure to adhere to these can result in penalties and fines for your company and may be accompanied by a consent order to address the violation. With the rise of RegTech companies such as KY3P (a product by S&P Global), CUBE, and Thomson Reuters, there are plenty of options to ensure no regulation is missed.

DCF.301 Identification and Monitoring of Emerging Risks

An emerging risk is a type of risk that is not known until it happens. Examples include cybercrimes, GDPR, and, more recently, the COVID-19 pandemic. Both companies and governments analyze the ever-changing landscapes to determine where and when risks may occur and create disaster recovery and continuity of business plans to address it when it happens. Another example is if a country publicly announces that it's looking into passing a new law that drastically shifts the status quo, a company must adhere to it within a set period.

1. Identifying an emerging risk can be realized by watching the news, social media, or government websites.

2. Develop a plan to address its impact on existing processes and how to quickly re-engineer them and implement them with as little to no impact as possible on the employees and clients. A recent example of this is

Apple tackling the emerging risk of the EU forcing them to align their lightning cable with the country's regulations and switch to the more universal USB-C connectors. In an article from The Guardian, I read that the firm's stance on deviating from proprietary connectors "stifles innovation rather than encouraging it." However, before the EU regulation went into effect, Apple viewed it as an emerging risk that would alter its product line and its potential impact on itself from a design perspective and the customer's perspective.

3. After an emerging risk is identified, it is monitored to understand its progress. Leveraging Regtech companies listed in DFC.300, watching the news, or reading reputable articles and news sources can aid monitoring.

4. Emerging Risks are then reported in weekly or monthly corporate decks to inform leadership and other stakeholders. When the emerging risk is realized, meaning it shifts from a potential risk to an actual risk, it's time to take action and execute your action plan.

DCF.3 COMPLIANCE & CONTROLS
EMERGING RISKS IDENTIFICATION & MONITORING MODEL
IDENTIFY ⇨ MONITOR ⇨ REPORT

DCF.302 Establish Ongoing Monitoring, Refresh, and Calibration of Controls

Before the rollout of ongoing monitoring controls, most companies provide risk assessments to be filled out for both vendor relationships and non-vendor activities. Based on each of the responses, which carry a specific weight, a score is ultimately given to provide those owners of the activities a tiered rating. This will trigger a set of existing controls set by the company that must be tested on a set frequency and archived for regulatory and audit purposes. This will lay the foundation for the governance over said activities performed under your role and pave the way for new controls to be set by yourself and your team.

After implementing the controls, you want to establish ongoing monitoring or frequent oversight of their performance. When dealing with KPIs and KRIs, it's important to review them monthly, quarterly, semi-annually, or annually to ensure they are performing as expected.

The Ongoing Monitoring Control Model can be a manual or automated process through a company's portal or system. It allows you to manage all your controls in a single area and track the results and if they were done on time based on the set frequency.

1. Test the controls by following the established process. All controls should be accompanied by a process model,

which should be used when testing.

2. Review the test outcomes; did they pass or fail?

3. After reviewing the outcomes, assess the impact; did they breach or fail? Depending on the importance of the control, if it fails, you may need to report it to senior leadership or even the board of directors.

4. Decide whether to open an issue or corrective action plan to bring the control back into a favorable, passing result and address the underlying issue. Establish relationships and collaborate with your risk management team, as they can also provide guidance on what to do with breaches or failures.

5. Revisit the situation and see if more work needs to be done or complete the ongoing monitoring of your controls for the review period.

Calibrating a control means isolating it outside your typical reporting, often putting it in a different section of a corporate deck to track and demonstrate whether it captures the risk. The Control Calibration Model follows a basic cycle:

1. Identify a new or existing control that will be in scope for calibration. Reviewing the upper and lower control limits will also be required if the control reports 100% passing for multiple weeks or months, as it could be a sign you aren't capturing the right sample size.

2. Definition of the measurement criteria. This will set the foundation for the control and how it will be measured. Understanding the answers to the below questions will help with the measurement criteria.
   - What does the control measure?
   - What is the population and sample size for the test?
   - What is the threshold for passing and failing?
   - What is the escalation process when a control breaches or fails?
   - How will you continuously capture evidence?

3. Calibrating a control is important because it allows you to test its effectiveness and ensure it captures the right data points, is repeatable, and provides accurate results.

4. Monitoring effectiveness during calibration. You can set any amount of time to monitor the control in calibration. Typically, companies use six consecutive weeks, but any period longer than three weeks is enough to get enough of a sample. It's best practice to report the progress separately from your existing controls and post the data in weekly or monthly operating decks, ensuring that management and the teams involved are

made aware of the status. Using six weeks as an example, any time the control fails in calibration the monitoring cycle must reset back to zero; yes... even if you're on week five! Once it passes, you can move it to implementation.

5. Implementation of the control. After the control successfully passes six consecutive weeks in a row, it's time to move it out of calibration and report on it with your existing set of controls. Keep an eye on the control and continue to monitor it; if it isn't working the intended way, discuss it with your stakeholders and put it back into calibration.

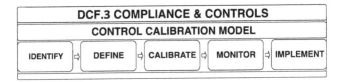

This systematic approach allows you to ensure the control is working appropriately, alerting you to the risk, and that the teams implementing it understand how to provide the necessary data for testing.

As stated, if a control continues to reflect 100% month-over-month, it may be time to reassess and refresh it to maximize its effectiveness. After you decide to refresh the control, it's time to put it into calibration. Once you successfully test and pass the control functionality, it's time to move it back into the regular reporting cycle; however, if it fails once, the six-week review cycle restarts.

DCF.4 Innovation

Innovation drives transformation. The ability to take something that exists today and build upon it to lessen the time spent on a process or to solve new problems is an important skill set to acquire. It can lead to increased motivation of employees and allow them to think outside the box to address long-standing issues tied to processes. Innovation doesn't have to be a grand idea but focusing on the small details to solve everyday problems. In a YouTube video, Simon Sinek discusses going to a retail store and looking at the toaster aisle to assess the lever on each model. There are $400 toasters that don't have the ability to lift the lever to easily get whatever you put in out, but a $30 toaster will. He says that is innovation. The ability to solve a minor problem to retrieve toast, bagels, etc., without sticking a knife in to get it out. Innovation is about driving things forward, identifying minor pain points, and providing solutions for ease of use.

At the time, when I worked for one of the largest financial institutions in the world, the organization I was a part of did not have a centralized vendor management program. They were all individually managed and sometimes felt like the Wild West. At the time, I was managing 14 vendors and saw an opportunity to take the same framework I developed and scale it to encompass the wider 221 vendors. This allowed for a centralized model that included financial, contract, and resource management. By rolling out the new framework, leadership immediately received it well, and I grew my career through the power of innovation.

Another example is when I recently took on a new role in compliance. I immediately entered the role and looked for ways to innovate. The role entailed managing the regulatory profiles for the 97+ countries, ensuring that regulatory content applies to the company, and decreasing the number of non-applicable content. Before I joined the team, they heavily utilized large Excel spreadsheets to communicate with chief country compliance officers and their deputies to identify what could be adjusted on their profile to fix the issues. This process, however, was time-consuming and put additional responsibility on the chief country compliance officers and their team, which I saw as an opportunity. I stepped back and went to the drawing board to see what could be done. I decided to take a data-driven approach and look at the last six months of data to see what on their profile could be enabled or disabled to reduce the noise and optimize the profiles. Within two weeks of being in the role, I had a concept and began socializing it. While it was a small change, innovation has led to a positive response from all stakeholders and yielded excellent results. Great ideas don't have to be big, but by listening to end users' pain points and struggles, you can make a lasting difference in their work.

DCF.400 Proactive Identification of Issues to Mitigate Risks

Proactively identifying issues to mitigate risks is an important skill when driving innovation. This stems from the question, "What is a risk?". Risk in business can be summarized as anything that threatens a company's financial goals. There are several types of risk, including reputational, geopolitical, concentration, and market, to name a few. When broken down at a process level, risk is anything that can go wrong that would cause the process to fail and, in return, impact the company's financial goals. Most companies have a slogan of "If you see something, say something," which not only applies to suspicious people but to risks that may not be known yet. The Issue Identification Model should be followed when driving process improvement or innovation.

1. Analyze the change being made as well as the end-to-end proposed process.

2. Assess the impact of implementation, such as if it is tied to other processes that may break, user error, or incompatibility with a system.

3. If you see something that needs to be adjusted or stopped to avoid a system outage or worse, report it to your management and follow your company's policies and standards.

DCF.4 INNOVATION		
ISSUE IDENTIFICATION MODEL		
ANALYZE ⇨	ASSESS IMPACT ⇨	REPORT

DCF.401 Strategy & Agility

A strategy is an overarching plan that sets the stage for companies, departments, and teams and what they will accomplish throughout the year, over many years, and when tackling process improvements. Strategies focus on the company-wide objectives and goals and how the direction will be laid out to accomplish them. Depending on your role, a strategy may be minimal or complex, with several projects and new functions or processes being rolled out. The Strategic Planning Model focuses on three key areas to develop and implement a great strategy.

1. The first stage of the model is to plan the strategy, considering the company-wide objectives and goals and understanding what needs to be completed and by when. This will constitute what some call a strategic roadmap. As part of the planning stage, the strategic roadmap draft will be taken for review and feedback from peers, your leadership team, and management.

2. Once everything is approved and agreed upon, it's time to understand what processes, new or existing, will need to be created or adjusted to meet the needs of the strategy. This is when the Dragonfly Construct comes

into play – taking each process through a methodical and systemic approach to capitalize on understanding the ins and outs of a process before it's created or re-engineered. It encompasses the Egg, Larva, and Adult Stages to understand your team and other departments' goals. From there, it's a matter of identifying the areas of opportunity and potential solutions and understanding interdependencies between all teams involved to ensure you don't break anything.

3. Implement the process. After everything is executed, take a step back to assess if anything needs to be adjusted.

The other key to delivering a successful strategic roadmap is ensuring you and your team have agility. No, not the ability to sprint a marathon without breaking a sweat, but the ability to pivot at a moment's notice to address any issues that pop up during the roadmap's execution. Proper agility allows your team not to get flustered or caught up on blockers but to press forward and begin to think outside the box to resolve the problem.

DCF.4 INNOVATION
STRATEGIC PLANNING MODEL
PLAN ⇨ UTILIZE THE DRAGONFLY CONSTRUCT ⇨ ASSESS

Whenever I interview for a new job or start in a new position, I create an operating model based on the Dragonfly

Construct's main objectives. This helps align my vision with the role and team and demonstrates critical and strategic thinking to interviewers and management. The out-of-the-box thinking gives you a competitive edge against candidates and your peers. Having a good strategy is more than putting what needs to be done on paper; forecasting what you'll steer the role or team and gives purpose. Speaking of purpose, the operating model should be accompanied by a purpose statement. What is the overall purpose of what you bring to the table, and how will you accomplish it? Perhaps it's solving a problem or building out a "best in class" function with the partnership and collaboration of peers, stakeholders, and other departments, such as risk management and audit. A simple two to three-sentence purpose statement can make all the difference when communicating your 'why.' It's become a positive habit I've developed over the years, leaving a lasting impression on those around me.

Case Study 4 – Implementing Frameworks

Audience: Organizations (offsite activity or general team building exercise) and Individuals (personal, high school, or college class activity).

Purpose: Using Chapter 5: The Dragonfly Construct Framework, select a company of your choice and implement the Dragonfly Construct framework. This will help you obtain a beginner-level understanding to develop a strategy for a small, medium, or large organization.

Structure: 1,500-2,500-word analysis

Process:

Step 1. Identification

1. Select an organization of your choice
2. What industry is it in?
3. What is the size?
4. Are you aware of any existing frameworks being utilized today?
5. Ask a family member, friend, or add/reach out to someone on LinkedIn and see how process improvement is made in their organization and how a framework would be rolled out

Step 2. Execution

1. At what level in the organization would you implement this framework?
2. Who would you present the framework to to receive proper buy-in? What barriers do you perceive you'd encounter?

Step 3. Detailed Analysis

Provide a detailed write-up with the area of opportunity, potential solution(s), analysis of the Dragonfly Construct Framework, proposed execution time, and a pitch deck.
Be sure to include the following:

1. The organization you selected, its industry, size, and why you chose it
2. Your understanding of the Dragonfly Construct Framework and the purpose of each key objective
3. How would you implement the framework across your selected organization; change management and strategic plans
   a. Develop a strategic roadmap with either a multi-month or year plan to introduce, train, gather feedback, and implement the framework
4. What controls you would put in place to measure the success of the framework, key objectives, and sub-objectives
5. Timeframe to implement the framework

Step 4. Check Your Understanding

Based on your analysis, include responses to the below questions:

1. What is the purpose of a framework within an organization?
2. How can you build consensus when sharing a new idea?
3. How do you handle conflicting feedback and viewpoints when sharing an idea?
4. What did you learn about integrating frameworks and creating a multi-month or year strategy to implement it?
5. How has your understanding of controls within the workplace grown through this activity?

CHAPTER 6

Getting it to Stick (A Reader's Metamorphosis)

The hardest part is getting everyone on board or driving consensus. No one is perfect, and we all know mistakes will happen, but do what you can to minimize the chances. It starts with you as the manager or employee. You must firmly believe that the process(es) you are changing will lead to a better outcome, whether time or cost-saving. Utilizing and teaching the Dragonfly Construct to your peers and managers will aid in creating an environment for solving complex solutions and improving processes around you. By leading by example, your team will pick up on it, slowly integrating it into their everyday interactions. Teach your employees, or yourself, to look at all processes through the lens of your users and stakeholders. As I said before, users and customers can pick up on that. There are ways of offering products and integrating new features that show that you care about them and want to provide a service to help them rather than just what has been done before. Just like you should put your employees first, they must put the end-user and stakeholders first, which will help you drive profits and process advancements. Encouraging others to dig deep and adapt to the world through process improvement is essential for personal growth and moving an organization forward. I know personally that changing processes is complex, from start to finish. However, it becomes second nature after you get the hang of it. This is a valuable skill as you navigate the workplace, and companies must have roles dedicated to process improvement and re-engineering.

Anyone can change a process; it's not rocket science... but learning the ins and outs of different types of process improvement can aid heavily in driving change. Many exist today, such as Kaizen, Six Sigma, and PDCA, to name a few. Now, we have the Dragonfly Construct to add to the mix. What sets it apart is its unique focus on mindsets and a systematic approach over six months to implement change. This is not a one-size-fits-all solution; it's a flexible framework that can be adapted to various scenarios, making it truly agile and transformational, like a dragonfly. If you have less time to implement a process due to multiple issues, you can still leverage the Dragonfly Construct, ensuring all interdependencies are known and approvals are in place. The Dragonfly Construct is both a process and mindset that provides a way to look at all the variables surrounding a process to deliver a sustainable solution for departments, organizations, and broader companies. Mastering process improvement is imperative to a team's success and pushing your critical thinking and strategic skills to the test.

When I created the Dragonfly Construct and gave my first TEDx Talk, I wasn't sure what to expect regarding feedback. Whether it was self-doubt or impostor syndrome, I didn't think I could produce a viable construct for people to improve processes in their daily lives and at work—and that they would actually use it.

The feedback I received and the Dragonfly Construct's impact on people was enlightening and melted my worries away. If even one person used it, I was successful in my mission. To further aid in getting it to stick and demonstrating the usefulness of the construct, I have compiled testimonials of people who have reached out after watching my TEDx Talk or reading my LinkedIn Posts on process improvement 'The Dragonfly Construct Chronicles' to inform me that they are leveraging the Dragonfly Construct at work and have had significant results.

Hunter Carrithers

Hunter started his professional journey after graduating from the Rawls College of Business at Texas Tech University and moving to Dallas. Today, he is 30 years old and has spent seven years in IT supporting recruitment, account management, and business development for digital engineering services. He is a husband, a father, and loves spending time with his family,

contributing towards Web3 initiatives, and learning about re-
generative agriculture. Hunter works at a fast-growing digital
engineering services firm partnering with over 30% of Fortune
100 companies in product/platform engineering, cloud, data,
and artificial intelligence & machine learning (AI/ML). The
company indexes talent and technology to deliver quality IT
talent fast and AI-powered platforms for greater transparency
and predictability on engineering spend.

Utilizing The Dragonfly Construct

"Taking the message and call-to-action from the framework,
I analyzed my sales team environment and the challenges we
were facing. My team had just endured the first few months of
a new logo change, which included an evolution and broad-
ening of our services. The learning curve was steep because
the services we now offered were a mix of talent and technology solutions that required a deeper knowledge of digital
engineering environments. As a non-technical salesperson, I
noticed a big gap in understanding our new company offerings despite stakeholder communications and training efforts.
New salespeople struggled to pick up on the technically heavy
language and concepts. Mature salespeople were not retaining the evolved concepts well, and the theory-based training
didn't allow for Q&A or situation-based practice. As someone with a natural strength at quickly picking up on new
technical concepts and being part of the sales team, I knew
this was a challenge I could positively impact. Through sales
meetings and "office gossip," I understood the detailed issues
salespeople in my area faced regarding this challenge. So, I first

approached my immediate manager during our one-on-one, explained the area of opportunity I saw, and asked for his feedback. After confirming we saw eye-to-eye on this issue, I asked him if I could take the initiative to schedule weekly sessions with the other salespeople in our office to start working on the issue. My suggestion was to give us allocated time to talk through recent client meetings, the nature of those meetings, the outcomes, and have us roleplay how they could have gone better. I also offered to create a "Jeopardy"-styled game that would be a fun, engaging way to retain the new concepts while increasing the number of micro roleplays we could all participate in. This took the theory-based training from stakeholders and put it into practice. My manager accepted my proposal and enabled me to schedule this weekly with the team. After just a few office sessions, the feedback I got was immediate and significant. Salespeople were getting a chance to ask questions, get immediate answers, and work through real scenario-based roleplays. In their words, this enhanced their ability to understand and retain new concepts.

A couple of weeks later, our CEO visited our office, and while we were at client meetings together, coincidentally, he asked how morale was and how the new company training was going. I shared with him the challenges I saw across the company, our solution to that at a local level, and the outcomes we've been experiencing. He was very excited and asked me how we could scale this initiative nationwide for all our sales regions. I told him each office could accelerate their confidence with these new concepts by enabling lead and senior salespeople to guide weekly roleplay sessions, leveraging the training materials and real-time sales activity situations. Then, as a supplement, once per month, we could record Zoom sessions with an engineering practice lead and upload those to a centralized repository so that any salesperson from the office could search and access roleplays based on specific topics. He was thrilled about this suggestion, and within two days, he scheduled a call with me and other company leaders to have me walk through my pitch in more detail. We brainstormed and eventually settled on a scalable practice-based training program that would be implemented nationwide and included in office metrics."

Andy Harper

Primarily growing up in the financial sector, with a focus on banking technology, project management, and a background in logistics, Andy serves as the Global Head of External Exams and Attestations for a significant risk team. He has over 20 years of IT Services experience focusing on agile leadership and risk reduction. Andy has a passion for learning, holding two ITIL V3, AWS Certified Cloud Practitioner, and Certified Scrum Master certifications, and has a Six Sigma Green Belt. As an ITIL and CSM technology enthusiast, Andy utilizes his technical and business knowledge to optimize business goals into tactical plans to reduce cost, mitigate risk, and streamline processes while collaborating with technology teams, stakeholders, and leadership to ensure optimal system implementations. Andy H. works at one of the top financial institutions in the world, operating in more than 160 countries and employing more than 230,000 associates.

Utilizing the Dragonfly Construct

"I love using the Dragonfly Construct throughout my daily interactions with my peers and partners. As part of conceptualizing opportunities, I use it to build an inclusive culture of improving transparency, streamlining collaboration, and maximizing our tools to reduce the needless complexity of processes while creating secure, reliable, and efficient results for our regulators and services for our clients and stakeholders. Through client interactions, I use it to help me better understand their requirements, where they are positioned, and where they would like to be in the near and long-term future. Understanding their vision, the Dragonfly Construct allows me to conceptualize building a roadmap to success to dynamically improve upon ideas from the 'think-tank' while identifying and removing existing wasteful processes. The Dragonfly Construct enables me to focus on implementing sound risk-preventative solutions for products or services in a simplified and cost-effective manner. As we move forward, we can quickly look across the landscape to identify other areas to apply these concepts and create a standard where cross-training new members or across small or large teams can commence."

Vivian Po

Vivian is no stranger to process improvement. She has held positions such as head of research & development, product management, learning and engagement consultant. She is currently the commercial lead for a tech-driven learning and development solution provider. Her passion and focus on making education accessible and relevant to careers and businesses aid in helping people find their niche and introducing process improvement elements along the way.

Utilizing the Dragonfly Construct

"I am actually at the end of the Adult Stage for my Sales to Operation streamlining process (cross-functional) and in the Adult Stage of Sales Process (in function). Your points are valid and crucial to meaningfully crafting a process, getting buy-ins, implementing it, and continuously improving it. This is a (for lack of better words) continuous effort simply because some processes are dynamic; we face situations requiring additional actions that may go against the process. When this happens, the stakeholders are caught off guard, which may cause inconveniences to the stakeholders involved.

One thing I realized about processes is that we need to be Agile, have empathy, and always understand the why."

Balasz Tumpek

Since 2015, Balazs Tumpek has worked for two of the largest American multinational investment banks. Both companies are on the Fortune 100 list with a presence worldwide, in 40+ countries with 80,000+ employees. They have profoundly embedded change into their culture and everyday life, and they evolve and transform like living organisms. Managing and embracing change is one of the lessons everyone learns at one point in their journey in this environment. Balazs is currently the Vice President of Divisional Data Quality and Control, managing data issues, policy implementation, and analytics.

Utilizing the Dragonfly Construct

"During the last eight years, I have been in seven different roles across three lines of business. I started in Identity and Access Management, then spent several years in Cybersecurity, Technology Risk Management, and Data Governance. With every new chapter, it felt like I was back to square one, and I wanted to get rid of this feeling as soon as possible. Trying to cut the learning time led to valuable lessons, such as why one should avoid rushing into projects.

Being new in a department, team, or role holds a wealth of opportunities if someone is patient enough. For me, the true potential of the Egg phase of the Dragonfly Construct is in accepting there will be a (limited) period where we won't feel like we're contributing. I learned to appreciate this observing mode when taking over the risk-related metrics and reporting for a global function. When we're talking about hundreds of data sources, understanding the mechanics might seem overwhelming at first. On day two, I had to put aside my expectation of becoming a subject matter expert and put on my learning hat. My answer to the weekly question is, "How are you going to automate reporting?" I openly had to say in the first couple of months, "I don't know...yet!". It was well worth sticking to the priorities of the Egg phase. By understanding the current state, I could propose a pathway for automation addressing the main pain points and improving efficiency.

As an engineer at heart, I enjoy the Larva phase. It means I get to take a process or a tool apart, understand how it works, and then put it back together (hopefully), improving it along the way. This approach also helps identify the purpose, why that thing exists, and opportunities for adding more value. Once I understand how we define and measure success, it is much easier to untangle the Gordian Knot of legacy processes around it. There's also the question if we're satisfied to do something just like it was done before. Maybe yes, due to time or resource constraints, but that will limit how much we can achieve. When I moved from one company to another, this habit helped me focus my energy and learn from something while improving it. To quote a friend, "Everything is good, and we're making it better."

Maturing to the Adult phase was not something I felt or noticed about myself. Looking back, the sign was generally that I could start to help others. When passing on knowledge starts to feel comfortable, it's a good sign that we are in the Adult phase. I think it's crucial that although we are at this latter part of the curve, whoever is joining they are at the beginning. Appreciating this helped me adjust expectations toward new joiners across multiple teams. Bringing somebody on board can mean we're teaching tasks. But if we want them to add value and innovate, they need time and support to go through each phase of the Dragonfly Construct.

If I had to summarize what the Dragonfly Construct gave me, I'd say it helped me manage my expectations whenever I started something new. Not saying I magically became patient enough...but maybe somewhat mindful of what I should focus on at a specific time to bring the most out of myself in a new challenge."

Valdir Campanini

Through the years, Valdir has performed many roles where an organizational transformation was required to support business strategy, generate innovation, and establish a feedback loop through continuous process improvement to maintain the business's competitive edge. Like Andy H. and myself, Valdir also works for one of the largest financial institutions in the world. Today, Valdir is the Global Head of Operational Health tied to one of the governance organizations responsible for overseeing the risk profile and focusing on audit, compliance, control testing, and continuous monitoring.

Utilizing the Dragonfly Construct

"With the Dragonfly Construct, I've been able to leverage a framework that allows me to quantify the effort towards the implementation of innovation, allowing the time required to acquire the knowledge by understanding the work being done into the level of details needed so the steps towards a process improvement can be discussed with the teams that will benefit from the improvements, ensuring adherence and fit for purpose. By leveraging the Dragonfly Construct, I achieved successful improvements at a global scale, standardizing services, reshaping how an organization operates, and supporting the organization's goals while reducing the risk footprint for daily operations."

Steve Lomeli

Steve Lomeli is a recent Canfield Business Honors Program graduate at UT Austin. He is a first-generation college student passionate about giving back to his community through education and technology. Professionally, Steve has worked as a software engineer at two of the largest American multinational technology companies, focusing on e-commerce, cloud computing, online advertising, digital streaming, and artificial intelligence. He has worked on applications used by millions of users throughout the world.

Utilizing the Dragonfly Construct

"Being early on in my career, I've found the Egg stage of the Dragonfly Construct to be the most applicable and beneficial. Entering a new professional environment always comes with its own set of challenges. Whether learning new processes from the ground up or simply networking with those around you and even those in more senior positions. However, as Jordan mentions, utilizing the "new joiner" card has never failed to help create a new connection or get a thorough run-through of a process.

Whenever I joined a new team, I would make it a point of

emphasis to talk to my peers performing similar work and to talk to my skip-level managers. These conversations would help set me up at the company by learning about current processes (along with their histories and pain points) or even "fairytale" processes for what an ideal world would look like. Often, I found that I'd get all of my "Why?" questions out of the way through these conversations, and thus, I was going into my role and duties with a much clearer understanding of it all. Beyond process-focused questions, these conversations helped me grow my professional network and become comfortable with those I worked with daily."

The Cycle Continues

Hearing stories from people who have integrated The Dragonfly Construct into their daily routine is great. When I started on this journey of creating a construct and a more comprehensive framework, I did not know what to expect, but it did solidify one thing. The ability to effectively challenge the status quo to drive process improvement is necessary to improve one's career and the processes you and your company utilize. Like the dragonfly, it is time for you to have your metamorphic journey and contribute to making a difference and transforming the workplace, people's lives, and the world around you.

For more information, check out evolvelikeadragonfly.com!

Call to Action!

Congratulations! You've made it to the end of the book. Hopefully, you are inspired and motivated to drive process improvement in your work or personal life. Take the time to reflect on the contents of this book and continue to revisit it as necessary to aid in challenging the status quo and implementing new solutions or improving existing processes.

If you've had success in implementing the Dragonfly Construct and want to share your story, drop me an email at Jordan@evolvelikeadragonfly.com

Afterword

Thank you to those who purchased this book. It's taken me over seven years to write and has gone through multiple iterations, and it truly means a lot. *Walk Among the Dragonflies* contributes to pursuing knowledge and generating new ideas through process improvement to change the world around you.

As a special thank you to the readers, a portion of every copy of *Walk Among The Dragonflies* sold is donated to the Neopte Foundation, Inc. The Neopte Foundation is a 501c3 nonprofit organization I started to provide purpose to youth from low-opportunity backgrounds with direction in pursuit of higher education for both university and trade school.

For more information, visit neoptefoundation.org

Acknowledgments

I wish to express my gratitude to those who encouraged me to continue pursuing greatness. The journey is not over as there is always more to learn and more work to be done.

To my wife, Elesia, who tirelessly put up with me and supported me from my academic career to immediately jumping into writing this book. You're the light of my life, and words can't even begin to explain how much I love and appreciate you.

I'd like to thank my dad, Steve Thurston, for being there every step of the way and helping me review and edit this book. Thank you for your support and patience through the writing process and for pushing me to dig deep and help me better express my thoughts and words. You offered so much wisdom and made great suggestions. Because of you, this book is better.

Thanks to my brother, Josh, who took time out of his busy schedule to create the internal graphics for the book. Your talent for art makes this book even more special.

I'd also like to thank my grandparents, Dennis & Cherry Ignatius, for continuously motivating and pushing me to strive for greatness. Taking time to review each chapter of my book and challenging me on certain topics helped to mold the book into what it is today. Being the grandson to an author of five books, I have more respect for the process and time put into it – and now I have a goal to surpass!

Special thanks to my mom, Leyna Ignatius, who consistently supported me through all my good and bad decisions – the verdict is still out for this book. Your sacrifices have paved the way for my success, and for that, I am grateful.

Special thanks to Linda Valloor, for not only proofreading my initial draft but for being an amazing world literature teacher who helped me expand my horizons and challenge the world around me through literature.

Finally, to my family, friends, managers, colleagues, mentors, and professors (in no special order): Mark Rose, Amy Thurston, Dave & Nina Nichols, Ella Nichols, Silas Nichols, Hannie Nichols, Jasmine "Mung Bean" Garza, John & Marcia Miller, Melissa Miller, Trey Miller, Anissa Miller, Tylan Miller, Judah Miller, Danny & Nassika Davila, Todd & Liz Miller, Paul Thurston, Paulo & MaryJane Thurston, Malcolm Smith, Naveen Baskar, Dharmesh & Preksha Mistry, Chris Moden, Christian & Haley Delcid, Jimmy & the late Lina Thurston, Jason & Missy Knechel, Fab & Kemberli Paes, Charles & Melissa Miller, Aaron & Monica Anderson,

Nicole Miller, Valdir Campanini, Andrew Harper, Balazs Tumpek, Hunter & Tatiana Carrithers, Stephen Zawolik, Dan McDowell, Ted Hernandez, Jennifer Kleinert, Paul Pitre, Mike Whitaker, Tony DiSanto, Sam & Veronica Kruger, Shadman Zafar, Sean & Whitney McAnallen, the late Paul Raines, the late Tony Bartel, Mike Dzura, James West, Chris Vessey, Samey Abdulrub, Zayn Abdulrub, Jalahni Robertson, Marcelo Ostria, David Simmons Jr., Robb Armstrong, Harki Dodia, Ben & Mai Manalang, Taylor & Karyn Elliott, John & Dianne Ricci, Donnie & Dara Petty, Brandon Bravo, Keith Meline, Josh Sylve, Eduardo Pastene, Nate & Katy Willingham, Tiffany Tran, Camryn Tanielian, Rahil Makani, Justin Gutierrez, Kerry Ao, Chris Conway, Rabih & Samantha Abi-Hanna, Phil & Adam Carls, Anh Le Palomino, Michael Brown, Josh Taino, Mihir Patel, Dean Catanzaro, Kyle De-Blonk, Dawn Flammang, Chad Barmettler, Matt Widders, Jim Adams, David Gong, Lung-Nien Lee, Eric Sim, Colin Smith, Mike Smith, Mike & Tina Tipton, Joe Longoria, Stephen & Misti Tucker, Andrew & Molly Christensen, Justin & Meagan Clemons, Dr. Marilyn Wiley, Dr. Brian Tietje, Dr. Josip Burusic, Dr. Mario Silic, Dr. Hrvoje Volarevic, Dr. Andreja Rudancic, Nick Bidinger, Dan Parker, Javier & Nikki Robles, Josh & Taylor Zuilkowski, Josh Cuello, Matt and Carrie Silver, Jody Triunfel, Jonathan & Jackie Robles, Stephen Connally, Art Lambert, Josh Cuello, Omar & Saxon Bhagat, Kristin Beideman, Tacy Valenteen, Jami West, Dr. Bill Clarkson, and countless others who either encouraged me in my journey or pushed me to *finally* write this book, your friendship and guidance is truly wonderful. It really takes a village.

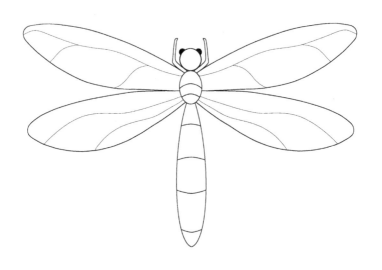

Printed in the USA
CPSIA information can be obtained
at www.ICGtesting.com
LVHW011655220624
783639LV00003BA/31